COLLECT

your

CHILD SUPPORT!

A STEP-BY-STEP GUIDE

TO COLLECT CHILD SUPPORT

FOR YOU AND YOUR CHILDREN

RICHARD W. TODD

ATTORNEY AT LAW

NATIONAL LEGAL SERVICES, INC.

PORTLAND, OREGON

COLLECT YOUR CHILD SUPPORT!
A STEP-BY-STEP GUIDE TO
COLLECT CHILD SUPPORT
FOR YOU AND YOUR CHILDREN

By: Richard W. Todd

Published By
NATIONAL LEGAL SERVICES, INC.
520 S.W. Yamhill, #430
Portland, Oregon 97204

Although the author and publisher have exhaustively researched all sources to ensure the accuracy and completeness of the information contained in this book, we assume no responsibility for errors, inaccuracies, omissions, or any inconsistency herein. Any slights of people or organizations are unintentional. Readers are encouraged to consult an attorney for specific applications to their individual situations.

Library of Congress Cataloging in Publication Data
Todd, Richard W. (Richard William), 1953 —
    Collect Your Child Support! A Step-by-Step Guide to
    Collect Child Support for You and Your Children / Richard W. Todd.

    224p. — cm.
    Includes Index

    ISBN 0-9636419-9-9 (pbk.)
    1. Child Support — Law and Legislation — United States — Popular works. I. Title.
    KF549.Z9T63 1994
    346.7301'72--dc20
    [347.306172]   93-44286
                                                                        CIP

CONTENTS

Introduction 3

Step One:

OBTAINING THE SUPPORT ORDER

1. **Paternity Actions** - What To Do If You
   Weren't Married to the Father............................ 11
2. **Divorce Actions** - How To Do It and How To
   Determine the Amount of Support......................17
3. **Modifying and Increasing Support** -
   How Much is Enough? 33

Step Two:

LOCATING THE ABSENT PARENT
(AND HIS MONEY)

4. **Attorneys and Attorney Fees** -
   When Do You Need Them;
   How Much Should You Pay?............................... 55
5. **How to Find the Absent Parent** -
   The Art of Skip Tracing..................................... 65
6. **Finding the Assets** - How To Get Results 87

I

Step Three:

COLLECTING THE MONEY

7. **Enforcement — Basic Collection Techniques -**
    Garnishment, Execution & Wage Withholding 105
8. **Using the Courts for Help -** Subpoenas,
    Debtor Exams and Contempt Hearings........... 125
9. **Using the Government for Help -**
    Title IV and the IRS... 147

Step Four:

SPECIAL SITUATIONS

10. **Collecting Money in Other States**
    and Countries 163
11. **Bankruptcy, The Military,**
    and Government Employees 181

CONCLUSION

Conclusion 197

Glossary.. 201

Appendix A 205

Appendix B 213

Appendix C 219

Index 221

Acknowledgment

I have not attempted to cite in the text all the authorities and sources consulted in the preparation of this manual. To do so would require more space than is available. The list would include departments of the Federal and State governments, libraries, periodicals and many individuals.

• Stevens Ness forms reprinted by permission.

Cover by Kerrie Tatone
Text by Arlene Opoka

"The duty of parents to provide for the maintenance of their children is a principal of natural law... by begetting them, therefore, they have entered into a voluntary obligation, to endeavor, as far as in them lies, that the life which they have bestowed shall be supported and preserved. And, thus, the children will have a perfect right of receiving maintenance from their parents.

...and if a parent runs away, and leaves his children, the church wardens and overseers of the parish shall seize his rants, goods, and chattels, and dispose of them toward their relief."

BLACKSTONE, 1750

1

INTRODUCTION

This book has a distinct attitude about child support collection. It is an attitude you should immediately start internalizing within yourself. That attitude is best expressed as follows: collection of money will only occur when it is more difficult for the absent parent to avoid you than to cooperate with you. In other words, the "squeaky wheel gets the grease." Although that statement may appear trite, it is the fundamental basis of successful child support collection.

Imagine for a moment that two collection agencies are pursuing you to collect money. One sends you a letter periodically from another state telling you that this is your "last chance" to "avoid more severe collection activity." The other collection agency calls you continuously, files a lawsuit against you, demands your presence in court to ask questions about your assets, has the sheriff take things that belong to you, takes money out of your bank account, and attaches your wages.

Which collection agency are you going to pay?

Don't be misled by the above example. This book is not about how to make harassing telephone calls or dunning letters. That is, in fact, how collection agencies often operate, but it will not be effective for you in the collection of child support. Once an absent parent learns that this is all you are going to do, the letters go in the garbage and the telephone number gets changed. This example is only used to demonstrate the importance of determination - the "attitude" - in successful collection actions.

This book is about being a squeaky wheel with teeth. It is about transferring the frustration of unsuccessful collection (you) to the frustration of unsuccessful avoidance (the absent parent). It is about forcing the debtor—the absent parent—to accept the concept that paying you is preferable to not paying you. Once that concept is learned, it normally is not forgotten. If it is, you can remind the person with the same measures once again. The muscle that you use to accomplish this "transfer of frustration" is the sum of all the legal tools that are available to you to collect money. With these tools, you don't need to make harassing telephone calls, send dunning letters, or waste time and energy on unproductive efforts. You don't need to sit back and wring your hands. Most importantly, you don't need to feel like a helpless victim.

Regardless of whether you use the government or an attorney to assist you, you need to take an active role in collection in the absence of voluntary payment by the absent parent. Most of you are probably aware that the government is required to assist you—at virtually no charge—in your collection efforts. However, most of you who have used the government are probably aware of the limitations of this assistance. As in many other areas of government, "government assistance" works better in theory than it does in practice. Nonetheless, government-assisted child support enforcement is a multi-billion dollar industry, and growing bigger every year. As a result, government agencies charged with assisting you will have even less time, energy, and resources for each individual case. Your role in the collection process will therefore become even more important if you want to be successful in collecting any money.

Hiring a lawyer to handle this problem is another avenue available, but for most of you will be out of the question. The average hourly rate for an attorney today exceeds $100 per hour. Most lawyers don't like support collection work and most don't know how to do it properly. There are areas where lawyers can be used for specific purposes and there are ways to have the absent parent pay the legal fees. There are also arrangements where the lawyer receives a percentage of what they collect. These situations are discussed in later chapters of this book. Rarely, however, can you turn over a difficult collection matter to a lawyer and come out ahead if you are paying the lawyer by the hour. Most of the time, when you contact a lawyer for support enforcement assistance, they will refer you to the local government support enforcement office. (This is usually true even for the attorney who handled your divorce.) It's not that they don't care about your situation; it is because they know that they cannot handle the case efficiently.

As a result of these and other factors, most custodial parents feel helpless to do much of anything to collect child support payments. Unless you understand the system, it is hard to make the system work for you. It is well documented that many absent parents fail to pay child support, court ordered or not. The lack of child support payments is a major cause of welfare dependency by single mothers. Even in those cases where child support was ordered, the average order amounts to only seventy percent (70%) of the poverty standard and constitutes only about one-quarter of the estimated normal expenses incurred in raising children. Almost all women who are not receiving support are living in poverty or close to it.

This problem is not unique to mothers who have custody. One in ten single-parent families is headed by a man. Most of them do not receive child support either. Even though this book refers to "absent fathers", the rules, procedures and strategies outlined in this book for support enforcement can work equally well against absent mothers. The reason this book is designed to assist custodial mothers, however, is that the bulk of the problems are with absent fathers who do not pay. There are between four and five million of you out there who are facing this situation.

This book is designed to assist you no matter where you are in the continuum of the collection process. Many of you were not married to the father. Some may have a support order, but the ordered amount of money is insufficient. Some may be in the middle of a divorce. One million of you have a support order, but have never received one red cent from your ex-husband or boyfriend. Wherever you are in the collection process, this book can assist you by describing the alternatives available to you, with or without a lawyer, and with or without the assistance of the government.

Basically, this book is divided into three parts. The first part is for those of you who do not have a court order for support. Obtaining a court order for support is the first step to enforce support and is essential; without it you are totally at the mercy and whim of the absent father as to when — or if — he wants to pay. With the court order, you can utilize the tools outlined in this book, enforce payment, and effectively transfer control of the amount and frequency of payments from him to you. Chapter One, therefore, tells you how to obtain such a support order if you were never married (a "paternity action"); Chapter Two describes how to obtain a support order if you were married to the absent father ("divorce"). Chapter Three is for those of you who have a support order but need or want to modify (increase) it. Millions of women have support orders that do not even begin to pay the expenses of raising children. Most of these orders were obtained long ago, before child support became a significant issue. Chapter Three discusses what your support order should be, and how to increase it if it is too low.

ONCE YOU HAVE ARMED YOURSELF

With a support order, you must locate the absent parent or his assets, preferably both. Collection is indeed difficult if you cannot find the absent parent to force him into court, or if you cannot find any money or assets to take to apply to the obligation owed you. Step Two of this book is therefore devoted to techniques for finding the absent parent and ways in which to locate his assets. It also includes a chapter on attorneys and attorney fees to assist you in evaluating whether you want to use them in this process, and alternative ways to pay them for their services.

Part Three is the most important step in the collection process: what to do when he doesn't pay, when he pays late, or when he doesn't pay the full amount. Or when he leaves the state, or refuses to work. Or files bankruptcy, or disappears entirely. Step Three is where you actually collect the money. It includes a chapter on basic enforcement techniques to obtain payment and how to use the courts for help through subpoenas, judgment debtor exams, and contempt hearings. It describes how you can use the government for assistance through Title IV and the Internal Revenue Service. All of these alternatives to enforce collection are explained so that you may select those procedures that are applicable to your particular situation.

Step Four covers those situations which are coming up more frequently in today's society. Special problems occur when the absent parent moves to another state or country to avoid collection. Chapter Ten describes those procedures available to you when such a situation occurs. Chapter Eleven details the process of collection from persons in the military and other types of government employees. It also outlines your rights and remedies should the absent parent file for bankruptcy, an occurrence that has increased in frequency over the last several years.

AS YOU READ THIS BOOK

You may think that some of the collection techniques described and recommended are harsh. Some of them are. Some can spell financial ruin for a self-employed businessman. All are at a minimum embarrassing and humiliating. One method, contempt actions, can result in imprisonment for the delinquent father. My response to this concern is an old joke about a farmer and his mule. They were on their way to the market and the farmer had hitched the mule to the wagon. Suddenly, the farmer walks up to the mule and hits him in the head with a sledgeham-mer. "Hey", said a shocked onlooker, "Why don't you use the buggy whip to get him to go?"

"I intend to" said the farmer. "I just have to get his attention first".

The techniques outlined in this book will get his attention. Although harsh, you must be prepared to use them. Hopefully, you will only have to use them once, but even using them once is a difficult decision to make. Keep in mind, however, that failure to pay child support is a crime; and failure to pay your child sup-port is a crime against both you and your children. Only by edu-cating yourself about child support and enforcement, and by using the techniques that you learn, can you protect yourself and your children against this crime.

That is the attitude of this book. It is the attitude you must adopt to be successful in collecting money. It is not an undertak-ing of the heart; emotions such as guilt, fear, sadness, etc. should play no part in what you are doing in this process. It is — strictly speaking — a business, the business of collecting money. I rec-ognize that eliminating your emotions in this process is easier said than done. But the more you can internally adopt this mindset — the attitude — the more successful you will be in collecting child support.

Obtaining the Support Order

PATERNITY ACTIONS

WHAT TO DO IF YOU WEREN'T MARRIED TO THE FATHER

In order to collect child support from an ex-spouse or former boyfriend, you must obtain a legal document from the Court spelling out the obligation he is to pay and how it is to be paid. This is referred to as a "support order". If you are married to the absent parent, you normally obtain this order of support as part of the divorce proceeding. If you are not married to the absent parent, you obtain this order through a "paternity proceeding". According to census bureau statistics, only about half of the women in the United States caring for children by themselves have legally binding support orders. It is imperative that you verify the existence of your order of child support; if no such order exists, you must take the steps to obtain one.

The obligation to pay child support exists whether you are married to the absent parent or not. The child support requirement is based on the father's relationship to his child and not on his relationship to you. If he is, in fact, the father of the child, the obligation to pay child support is automatic. The only question is how much he will have to pay.

You cannot get an order of child support against a person until he either admits that he is the father or he is proved to be the father. If you are married to that person, he is presumed to be the father and nothing further need be proven; the divorce action will address the issue of child support as part of the same proceeding (See Chapter 2). If there is no marriage, there will of course be no divorce proceeding. You must file a paternity action if the man will not admit he is the father of your child.

Since 1968, children born out of wedlock (i.e., born of two people who are not married) have the same rights as other children and are protected from wrongful discrimination by the Equal Protection clause of the U.S. Constitution:

> "We start from the premise that illegitimate children are not "non-persons". They are human, live, and have their being. They are clearly "persons" within the meaning of the equal protection clause of the Fourteenth Amendment."

This declaration by the United States Supreme Court terminated the long-standing rule in this country that allowed a father to walk away from the children he sired with no duty of support.

In virtually all states today, a person can acknowledge he is the father of a child by signing a written admission called a "consent agreement". When eventually confronted with this issue, most fathers will admit it and not fight the issue in court. This consent agreement is thereupon filed with the court and officially establishes paternity.

Establishment of paternity is the only way to force the father to assume legal responsibility for the child when the parents are not married. It may also be required in some states if you were married but living apart when you became pregnant. Establishment of paternity will make child support payments an absolute right among other rights, including: medical and life insurance benefits, social security, possible veterans benefits, and rights to inheritance. Most importantly, however, the child knows that he has a father (even if he is a deadbeat) and feels more complete.

Legal Services Are Free

For reasons to be explained in later chapters of this book, you should file for paternity and child support even if the father has no money or his whereabouts are unknown. No one knows what the future will bring, and the legal services available to assist you in establishing paternity are free; you might as well take advantage of it while you can. Also, there may be time limits to bring these types of actions (statutes of limitation) that may prevent you from bringing a paternity action in the future.

Historically, paternity cases were long, exhausting, and oftentimes sordid affairs. Accusations and cross-accusations overwhelmed the jury and the mother's virtue was repeatedly bantered about the courtroom. Such situations are uncommon in present-day paternity actions because of the accuracy of blood tests and other genetic procedures that can determine fatherhood with 99.99% accuracy. Faced with scientific evidence establishing the person with almost absolute certainty as the father of your child normally results in him agreeing to paternity. Full-fledged jury trials on this issue are a rare occurrence in today's society. Attorneys for the putative (alleged) father normally focus their energies on negotiating the amount of child support rather than denying paternity when faced with this virtually incontrovertible scientific evidence.

The easiest and obviously the cheapest way to establish paternity is to contact your local child support enforcement agency. These offices are listed in Appendix A at the back of this book. They will ask you to fill out an application requesting information about the alleged father, the facts about your relationship with him, your pregnancy, and the birth of your child. Answers to these questions are kept confidential.

The caseworker will contact the putative father to see if he admits paternity. If he does, a consent agreement will be drafted and a court order will be prepared incorporating the consent agreement with an order awarding child support. If he denies being the father, a paternity action will be filed against him and he will be required by law to undergo genetic tests (blood tests) as will you and your child. Depending on your income, you may be asked to help pay for these blood tests (generally a few hundred dollars). In some states, the father may be required to take the blood tests. The blood tests, because of their accuracy, can virtually always determine who is the father and who is not. This is the primary reason so few of these cases actually proceed beyond this step.

With that in mind, do not be frightened off if a man denies paternity and requests a jury trial. If this situation occurs, the government attorney will represent you or you can retain your own private attorney if you so desire. Evidence is introduced by both sides and a jury or judge will review the evidence and make a decision. These can be unpleasant and the father's attorney will often times try to intimidate you by threatening such a trial by jury. Do not be intimidated by such a maneuver; it is probably just a bluff. Keep in mind at all times that you are doing this for the benefit of your child and seek the support of friends and relatives to help you endure it.

If the putative father refuses to consent to paternity or consent to the blood tests, the court will issue a paternity court order anyway. If the blood tests are positive in showing that he is the father of the child, the court will order child support in spite of the fathers continuing objections. The only way that the putative father can avoid a paternity order and subsequent payment requirements is to take the blood test and be declared not to be the father.

The consent agreement or paternity order will spell out how much child support is to be paid and where and when payment is to be made. The amount is identical to the amounts awarded in divorce actions where the parties were married. The specific way to calculate the child support amount is set out in Chapter Two. These orders generally do not include visitation of the child unless so requested by the father. If you are uncomfortable with the father visiting the child, you can request the court to order supervised visitation only. Other parental rights can also be specified; if no agreement is reached, the court will decide at a formal hearing. Once the paternity order is entered, all rights and remedies will be available to you to enforce the child support order.

One final note. Statistically three fourths of married women obtain child support awards while only twenty five percent (25%) of mothers who never marry obtain such an award. If possible, establish paternity at birth (the "happy hour") when proud fathers are most likely to acknowledge their fatherhood and accept their parenting obligations.

CHAPTER TWO

DIVORCE ACTIONS

HOW TO DO IT AND HOW TO DETERMINE THE AMOUNT OF SUPPORT

If your child was born during your marriage, your husband is presumed to be the father of the child. To obtain an order requiring him to pay child support requires you to file a petition for divorce. Although in some states you can sue for support without filing for divorce (for example, formal separation agreements), such a proceeding is rare and in some states not allowed. Accordingly, we will discuss only the conventional divorce action.

A divorce accomplishes the following:
1. It formally terminates your marriage.
2. It determines how your personal and real property shall be divided between you.
3. It can change your last name, if you so desire.
4. It orders the payment of any spousal support (alimony) if appropriate.
5. It awards attorney fees to either side, if appropriate.
6. It orders the payment of child support.

Included in the order to pay child support will be the amount that is to be paid, where it is to be paid, and a determination as to which party gets the tax exemption for the child or children when filing federal and state income tax returns.

Basically, filing a petition for divorce is like filing a lawsuit against your husband. You must prepare a petition for divorce and file it in the county where either you reside or your husband resides. A copy of this complaint that you file is served on your husband by either the sheriff or a private process server. This petition generally contains your request for relief: the fact that your marriage has broken down and you want a divorce, the personal and real property you feel you should be awarded, the amount of spousal support you feel your husband should be required to pay, and a request for child support. The amount of child support is generally not determined by the petition but is established by statutory guidelines in every state (discussed later in this chapter).

The exact format to follow in preparing the petition varies from state to state but it basically is designed to provide the family court with a summary sketch of you and your husband, the children involved, the personal and real property that you own and a short statement setting forth the essential facts which demonstrate a duty of support. A sample petition for divorce is set forth on page 20 through 21.

FILING FOR DIVORCE IS A RELATIVELY SIMPLE PROCEDURE

The format varies little from case to case, and numerous kits and self-help publications are available to assist you in filling out the forms in the state in which you reside. As will be discussed later, statutory guidelines are in place in all states which set the amount of child support. This makes computation a simple process.

Once you file the petition, what happens next is up to your husband. If he fails to file a written response with the court within the appropriate time period (usually 30 days), you can file a motion for a "default" and obtain a decree of divorce. A motion for default is merely a request that the court sign the decree because there has been no response to your petition for divorce even though he has been served with a copy of your petition. Proof that your husband has been served with a copy of the petition needs to be filed with the court by the sheriff or process server. The judge will then sign an order of default and, after a brief hearing, sign the decree. In some states there is a waiting period ("cooling-off" period) before the Judge signs the decree or before the decree becomes final. The decree basically recites the information contained in the divorce petition, formally ends your marriage, awards the real and personal property you requested to you, and sets forth the child support obligation and how it is to be paid.

A sample motion and order of default and decree of divorce is set out on pages 21 through 22.

If your husband files a response to your petition, you cannot normally obtain a divorce decree by default. However, if you and your husband can agree on how the assets are to be divided, the amount of child support, etc., you can enter into a settlement agreement. This agreement is then reviewed by the court and made part of the decree of divorce ending your marriage. If the court feels that the settlement agreement is manifestly unreasonable with respect to the children, the judge may not allow it to be incorporated into the agreement. The Court may request that you and your husband appear at a hearing to ask you questions regarding your intents surrounding the settlement agreement. For example, if the amount of child support that you agree to accept is ridiculously low (say $25 per month), the judge may not approve it.

SAMPLE 1. PETITION FOR DIVORCE

IN THE CIRCUIT COURT OF THE STATE OF OREGON
FOR THE COUNTY OF MULTNOMAH

In the Matter of the Marriage of   )
) Case No. 5001

JANE DOE,
Petitioner,
)
)
) PETITION FOR
) DISSOLUTION
) OF MARRIAGE
)

JOHN DOE,
Respondent.
)

Petitioner alleges:
1.

The parties were married in Douglas County, Oregon, on May 1, 1982, and have ever since been husband and wife.

2.

Irreconcilable differences between the parties have caused the irremediable breakdown of their marriage.

3.

No other domestic relations suit or support proceeding involving the parties or any dependents of this marriage is pending in any court.

4.

Petitioner has been a resident of Oregon for six continuous months immediately prior hereto.

5.

Respondent is not a person in the military service of the United States of America or its allies and is not subject to the provisions of the Soldiers' and Sailors' Relief Act. Respondent is neither a minor nor an incapacitated person.

6.

There is one child of the marriage, namely: Tammy Doe, born April 15, 1987.

Petitioner is not pregnant.

Petitioner has not participated as a party, witness or in any other capacity in any other litigation concerning the custody of the minor child in this or any other state,

7.

Petitioner should have custody of the parties' minor child subject to reasonable visitation by Respondent.

8.

Respondent should pay a reasonable amount toward the support of the parties' child.

9.

The parties are owners of certain personal property, equitable division of which should be made by the Court.

10.

The parties have incurred debts during their marriage, the payment of which should be assigned as may be just and proper.

11.

Respondent should be required to pay Petitioner's reasonable attorney fees, together with court costs incurred herein, pursuant to ORS 107.105(1)(i), if this matter is contested.

12.

Petitioner's name should be changed to Smith, a former legal name.

WHEREFORE, Petitioner prays for a judgment:

1.Dissolving the marriage of the parties.

2.Granting other relief in conformance with the allegations of this Petition.

3.Granting other appropriate equitable relief.

Respectfully submitted,

SAXON, MARQUOIT & BERTONI
Richard W. Todd, OSB #79421
Of Attorneys for Petitioner

SAMPLE 2:   MOTION AND ORDER OF DEFAULT

IN THE CIRCUIT COURT OF THE STATE OF OREGON
FOR THE COUNTY OF MULTNOMAH

In the Matter of the Marriage of	)	
	)	Case No. 5001
JANE DOE,	)	
	)	
Petitioner,	)	MOTION AND ORDER
	)	OF DEFAULT
and	)	
	)	
JOHN DOE,	)	
	)	
Respondent.	)	

THIS MATTER coming on regularly to be heard at this time before the above-entitled Court, Petitioner appearing by Affidavit and Respondent not appearing, and

IT APPEARING to the satisfaction of the Court from the records and files of this cause that Respondent was served by personal service in the State of Oregon, County of Multnomah, on the 10th day of June, 1993, and that the time allowed for by law for answering said Petition has expired.

NOW, THEREFORE, IT IS HEREBY ORDERED, ADJUDGED AND DECREED that said Respondent be, and hereby is, declared to be in default for want of an appearance and the clerk of the Court is hereby ordered to enter said default in the manner provided for by law.

DATED this _____ day of June, 1993.

IT IS SO MOVED:

_____   _____
Petitioner   CIRCUIT COURT JUDGE

SAMPLE 3:   DECREE OF DISSOLUTION OF MARRIAGE

IN THE CIRCUIT COURT OF THE STATE OF OREGON
FOR THE COUNTY OF MULTNOMAH

Department of Domestic Relations

In the Matter of the Marriage of)	
)	
JANE DOE,)	No. 5001
)	
Petitioner,)	DECREE OF
)	DISSOLUTION OF MARRIAGE
and)	
)	
JOHN DOE,)	
)	
Respondent.)	

THIS MATTER having come on for hearing before the above-captioned Court and the Court finding: that it has jurisdiction in this matter; that the parties were married on May 1, 1982, in Reedsport, Oregon; that there has been one child born of this marriage, namely Tammy Lyn Doe, born on April 15, 1982, and petitioner is not now pregnant; that irreconcilable differences between the parties have caused the irremediable breakdown of the marriage; and the Court being fully advised in the premises, NOW, THEREFORE,

It is hereby ORDERED, ADJUDGED and DECREED as follows:

1. The marriage of the parties is hereby dissolved, such dissolution being final and effective the 30th day of December, 1993.

2. The parties shall share joint legal custody of the minor child of the marriage, with physical custody being granted to petitioner subject to respondent's rights of visitation as follows:

a. Respondent shall enjoy reasonable and seasonable visitation with the minor child.

3. Respondent shall pay to petitioner as child support for the minor child of the parties the sum of $300 per month, to commence on November 1, 1993 and on the first day of each month thereafter, until said child achieves majority, becomes self-sufficient or is otherwise emancipated; EXCEPT that said support obligation shall continue until the child reaches 21 years of age if that child is a "child attending school" as defined in statute.

4. Respondent shall pay any indebtedness incurred during the marriage and hold petitioner harmless on the obligations so assumed. Each party agrees to pay all other debts incurred by that party since the separation of the parties and to indemnify and hold the other harmless therefrom.

5. Both parties shall provide for the benefit of the minor child whatever health insurance coverage is available through their respective employments.

6. Except as allocated above, each party shall be awarded all personal property currently in that party's possession, free of any right, title or interest of the other.

DATED this_____ day of _____, 199__.

_____
CIRCUIT COURT JUDGE

In a settlement agreement, everything is negotiable. The thing to keep in mind at all times when negotiating a settlement agreement is your interests and the interests of your children. Remember that, unless there is a substantial change in circumstances, this will be the agreement you must live by until your children reach the age of majority. Your living expenses, your children's living expenses, and your children's special needs must be considered. It is difficult to come back later and change the agreement if you forget something. Even if you reach an agreement that you are comfortable with, I strongly encourage you to have an attorney review the agreement even if he does not represent you in the divorce proceeding itself. The relatively small amount you will pay for this review is greatly outweighed by the headaches you may encounter in the future as a result of over-looking some detail.

Settlement agreements have no prescribed form or structure. The example on page 25 is designed to provide you with a suggested format and to point out issues that you may overlook.

If your husband files a response with the court, and if you are unable to agree on the terms of your divorce (such as child support amount or division of assets), then the case is scheduled for a trial or hearing. If you find yourself at this stage of the proceeding, I recommend that you obtain an attorney to represent you if you do not already have one. This is especially true if your husband is represented by an attorney. It is very difficult to participate in a trial when representing yourself. I have seen many people do it, including attorneys, and it is very awkward.

It can be done, however, and you may have no choice. The judge will swear you in as a witness, and you will tell the court what you want and why you want it. If the judge has any questions, he or she will ask you. One way or the other, you will end up with a divorce and an order of child support if no one disputes you having custody of the children. If that is not the case, and your husband is requesting custody, it is imperative that you have a lawyer represent you. Otherwise, the risk is very real that you will lose custody of your children and be required to pay him child support.

As discussed in Chapter One, you should not let your inability to afford an attorney prevent you from getting an order of child support through a divorce action. There are numerous low-cost and free legal assistance programs available to you in your area. Consult Appendix B for persons to contact locally for assistance.

SAMPLE 4

IN THE CIRCUIT COURT OF THE STATE OF OREGON
FOR THE COUNTY OF MULTNOMAH

Department of Domestic Relations

In the Matter of the Marriage of	)	
	)	
JANE DOE,	)	No. 5001
	)	
Petitioner,	)	
	)	PROPERTY SETTLEMENT
and	)	AGREEMENT
	)	
JOHN DOE,	)	
	)	
Respondent.	)	

THIS AGREEMENT made and entered into this _____ day of
_____, 1993, by and between JANE DOE, hereinafter referred to
as "Wife" or "Mother", and JOHN DOE, hereinafter referred to as "Husband"
or "Father";

WITNESSETH:

WHEREAS, irreconcilable differences between the parties have
caused the irremediable breakdown of the marriage; and

WHEREAS, the Wife, a Petitioner, has filed a Petition in the Circuit
Court of the State of Oregon, praying for a dissolution of marriage, together
with other matters; and

WHEREAS, the parties have agreed upon a full settlement of all their
respective property rights and interests, subject to Court approval;

NOW, THEREFORE, in consideration of their mutual promises here-
in contained, the parties stipulate and agree that in the event a Decree dissolving the marriage is granted in the proceedings now pending, and subject to the
approval of the Court, the rights of the parties shall be settled and disposed of
as follows:

1.

A. One child has been born of this marriage. Respondent shall pay
to Petitioner $300 per month for the support of said child.

2.

A. The parties own certain real property located at 0000 S.E.
Madison, Portland, Multnomah County, Oregon, identified as Tax Lot No. 00
and more particularly described as follows:
Lot 00, Block 00, Sunnyside Addition in the City of Portland, County of
Multnomah and State of Oregon.

B. The above described real property shall be awarded to Wife free
and clear of any claim, right, title and interest of Husband. Wife shall assume

all mortgages, property taxes, maintenance and any other indebtedness on the real property and shall hold Husband harmless therefore. To effect the transfer of Husband's interest in said real property to Wife, he shall execute a Bargain and Sale Deed and deliver same to Wife within thirty (30) days of date of entry of this Decree.

3.

A. Husband is hereby awarded a certain 1978 Ford pick-up, free and clear of any right, title or interest of Wife, and shall hold Wife harmless from any indebtedness thereon.

B. Wife is hereby awarded a certain 1987 Ford Granada, free and clear of any right, title or interest of Husband, and shall hold Husband harmless from any indebtedness thereon.

4.

The parties own certain personal property, household goods, furnishings and appliances, clothing, bank accounts and pension benefits. Each party shall be awarded as his/her sole and separate property all such personal property in his/her possession.

5.

The parties mutually agree that in the event a Decree of Dissolution shall be granted either of the parties hereto, that this Agreement shall be incorporated in said Decree and enforced as part of said Decree. Each party, on the request of the other party, will execute such instrument as may be convenient to carry out the terms of this Agreement. For failure of either party to carry out any term of this Agreement, or to execute appropriate documents of title in furtherance hereof, this Agreement shall act in lieu of such document of title.

6.

Petitioner and Respondent agree that any and all property hereinafter acquired by either party shall be the separate property of the one so acquiring the same, free and clear of the claim of the other, and Petitioner and Respondent hereby grant to the other all such future acquisitions of property as the separate property for the one so acquiring the same.

7.

If any suit (EXCEPT FOR THE PENDING DOMESTIC RELATIONS SUIT), action or other proceeding or appeal from a decision therein is instituted to establish, obtain or enforce any right resulting from this agreement, the prevailing party shall be entitled to recover from the other party, in addition to the costs and disbursements, such additional sums as the court may adjudge reasonable as attorney fees, both in the trial and the appellate court.

JANE DOE	Date
Petitioner	

JOHN DOE	Date
Respondent	

DETERMINING THE AMOUNT OF
CHILD SUPPORT TO BE PAID.

Stories abound regarding unfair and outrageous child sup-port awards on both sides of a dispute. Cases in the past where wealthy fathers were ordered to pay only $50 a month were not uncommon, nor were cases where fathers were ordered child sup-port amounts that exceeded their monthly income. Because of this variety and inconsistency, federal legislation was passed in 1989 to make child support awards more uniform, more fair, and more realistic. All states now have child support guidelines based on the incomes of both the mother and father. If either or both parents have no income, an income is imputed to them for the purpose of establishing a child support amount. The court must follow the guidelines in setting a child support amount unless the judge sets forth in writing why the guidelines should not be fol-lowed. These guidelines supposedly represent the consensus of experts in the field as to what it costs to support a child, the needs of the child, and the ability of the noncustodial parent to pay based on his or her needs and expenses. It is a compilation of averages: the average needs of the average child and the average expenses of the average custodial parent coupled with the average needs and expenses of the non-custodial parent.

Your situation may be different. Proving such a difference entitles the court to deviate from the guidelines and adjust the child support obligation upward or downward. For example, a child may have special medical needs which require the purchase of medication in the amount of $200 per month. Based on this additional expense (and assuming it is not covered by health insurance), the judge could adjust the child support figure higher than the guidelines to compensate for this special need.

Two basic types of guideline formulas are used in the United States: guidelines based on a percentage of the non-custodial par-ent's income, and guidelines based on the combined income of both parents.

Guidelines based on the non-custodial parent's income are the easiest to compute. Wisconsin, for example, calculates the percentage based on gross income. A parent who has one child pays seventeen percent (17%) of his gross income for child support. If he has two children, he pays twenty five percent (25%) of his gross income. Three children is twenty nine percent (29%), four children is thirty one percent (31%), and more than four children is thirty four percent (34%) of his gross. Delaware, on the other hand, bases the percentage on net income of the parents: one child is eighteen percent (18%), two children are twenty seven percent (27%), three children are thirty five percent (35%), four children are forty percent (40%), five children are forty five percent (45%), and six children is fifty percent (50%) of the non-custodial parent's net income.

Other states combine the income of both parents and use a chart to determine the expenses of raising children based on that income amount. This amount is then divided between the parents proportionately based on their relative gross income. Oregon is representative of this approach and is used in the following example:

Mother's monthly earnings:	823.00
Father's monthly earnings:	2,650.00
Combined monthly earnings:	3,473.00
Percentage share of income (Mother):	13.7%
Percentage share of income (Father)	76.3%
Basic child supp. obligation(Appendix D)	488.00
Child Care Costs (from Appendix D)	170.00
Total child support obligation	658.00
Mother's child support obligation	155.95
Father's child support obligation	502.05

In the above example, the father would have to pay $502.05 as his total child support obligation if he was not the custodial parent. If he received custody of the child, the mother would have to pay $155.95 to him for child support.

You will also note in this example that a child care cost was included with the basic child support obligation. Increasingly in all states, the cost of child care is being added on to the monthly child support obligation as a matter of right. If your state does not automatically calculate the child care cost, it should always be mentioned if relevant to justify an upward departure from the guideline. In other words, if you have to pay child care costs on top of everything else, the absent parent should share in that expense in addition to monthly child support obligations.

The support computation worksheet to calculate child support, the worksheet to calculate child care credits, and the schedule of basic child support obligations vary, of course, from state to state. Some states have officially recognized that older children are more expensive than younger children and have, accordingly, adjusted their guidelines. The child support guidelines used in your state can be obtained from the clerk of the court where family law matters are handled or from your local child support enforcement agency (See Appendix A).

If the absent parent is unemployed, his gross income is normally based on what he would receive if he worked for minimum wage full time (approximately $750 - $800 per month). If you can prove that he voluntarily quit his job in order to reduce the amount of child support, the judge can order the child support based on what he earned before he quit. If he is self-employed and you are unable to determine what his income is (or don't believe him), you can subpoena the appropriate business records to establish his gross income in the past. (More on that in Chapter Eight.)

For most people, the guideline amounts are appropriate and serve their purpose of simplifying what used to be a totally uncertain procedure. What follows is some of the more common reasons to justify a departure from the guideline amounts. If they fit your situation, they should be considered in either your negotiations or your presentation to the court.

- Remarriage of either party.
- Steady employment of the child.
- Poor health or decreased earning ability of either parent.
- Either parent reentering college or vocational school.
- Unforeseen financial crisis.
- Bonuses or profit sharing contribution by employer.
- Substantial net worth of either party.
- History of low earnings and/or under-achiever.
- Psychological therapy.
- Costs of litigation.
- Pre-school and child care.
- Misconduct of either party.

Child support payments are not tax deductible to the non-custodial parent. They are also not taxable as income to you. Because of this, the absent parent often argues that he should be entitled to the tax exemption for the children when filing the federal and state income tax returns. This is negotiable between you and your former mate and should be included in the order. If not, the custodial parent is presumed to be entitled to the exemptions.

Medical and life insurance should also be included in the order and is in addition to the child support payment. At a minimum, the absent parent should be required to include the children on his medical insurance if it is available to him through his work. This is a very common provision in child support orders and should not be overlooked. If health insurance by the father is not available, this is grounds for an upward adjustment from the guidelines in setting the child support amount. Similarly with life insurance; in the event of his death, you will receive no further child support. The children should, therefore, be named as beneficiaries on a term life insurance policy. If not, you should request an upward departure from the guidelines to reflect the cost of a life insurance policy insuring the life of the absent parent for the benefit of the children.

Finally, you should consider the manner of payment. In most states today, payment is made to a centralized governmental agency to insure an accurate accounting of payments received and payments owed in the event of a dispute over child support payment arrearages. This procedure, although it can cause a delay in receiving your child support payment, is usually to your benefit for several reasons.

First of all, the records kept by the governmental agency are presumed accurate. You do not have to keep track of cancelled checks, bank deposits, etc., resulting in a considerable time savings for you. Secondly, if the absent parent fails to pay, the agency will generally send a notice to the absent parent regarding his delinquency. This normally will get his attention faster than any complaints by you. Finally, and most importantly, these agencies are increasingly being given the power to automatically review the child support payments periodically to determine if they should be increased. This will only occur if the payments are being made through their offices. The significance and importance of this development will become clearer after you read the next chapter.

CHAPTER THREE

MODIFYING AND INCREASING CHILD SUPPORT

HOW MUCH IS ENOUGH?

I f you feel that the child support payments awarded to you in the divorce decree are inadequate, you may request that the Court increase them. Generally, you must show that there is a sufficient change of circumstances in your and your children's life from the date of the divorce decree that justifies an increase in support. If your decree does not provide for any child support to be paid to you, you may request that the decree be changed to allow for child support, whether there has been any change of circumstance or not. You may also have available to you an administrative review of your child support, regardless of any change of circumstances, if it has been at least two years since the date of your divorce.

Requests for increased child support are called "modification proceedings" and are available to your ex-husband as well. If he can show that his financial circumstances have deteriorated through, for example, illness or injury, he may successfully argue that his child support obligation should be decreased. It is important, therefore, to be mindful at all times that a modification proceeding can be a two-edged sword; it can backfire on you and result in a decreased child support award instead of an increase. Analyze objectively your current financial situation and whether it is sufficient under the law of modification to support an increase in child support.

THE LAW OF MODIFICATION

Generally speaking, your divorce decree will set forth the amount of child support your ex-husband is required to pay to you. Any modification of that child support amount can only be accomplished by proving that a change of circumstances has occurred since the time of your divorce. You have the burden of proving to the Court that the change of circumstances is sufficient to justify an increase in your child support award.

The Court only has the power to modify the support payments due in the future. They do not have the power to increase child support payments which were due prior to your filing the motion to modify. Support payments due after a motion to modify has been filed — but before the hearing — may be modified at the discretion of the Judge. In other words, the sooner you file your motion to modify, the sooner the increase in child support can take effect, regardless of when the hearing on the motion occurs. The decision of the Judge will generally relate back to the time of filing.

Example:

Wife receives a child support award on January 1, 1990, for $100.00 per month. In February, 1990, wife loses her job and is unable to find other employment. On May 1, she files a motion to modify the child support to $200.00. The hearing to increase the child support is heard by the judge on August 1, 1990. The Court could properly increase the child support retroactively commencing May 1, 1990, the date the motion was filed, but not prior to that time, even though the wife lost her job in February.

Another situation that frequently occurs is when a parent does not obtain an order of child support at all. The parent can bring a motion to modify the decree to require the father to commence making child support payments. However, it will only commence at the time of the filing of the motion; she cannot generally bring an action for contribution for amounts she has spent on the children in the past. In a recent case deciding this issue, the father was to pay child support in an amount to be agreed upon at a later date. The mother raised the children for 16 years and the father paid a total of $195.00 for the children's support. The mother filed a lawsuit against the father to collect child support for the previous 16 years and the trial court entered a judgment against the father for $10,000.00. The Court of Appeals reversed the trial court's decision, concluding that she could not sue for contribution prior to the filing of a motion to modify the decree.

The motion to modify the decree to increase child support does not suspend or excuse the father from paying the support previously ordered until the hearing before the Court. The children are entitled to receive the level of support set by the prior decree unless and until changed by a court order. The modification the court orders can be retroactive to the date of filing of the motion. Additional amounts would then be due and are set out in the modification order signed by the judge.

CHANGES IN CIRCUMSTANCES

So what is a change of circumstance sufficient to justify a change in child support? Simply put, the larger the contrast between the circumstances now and the circumstances at the time of the prior court order, the better the chances of success in meeting the burden of proving change. The trial court has broad discretion in determining whether you have met the burden of proving a material and substantial change in circumstances. The more factors of change that you can show, the better your chances of success. The following are the most important.

CHANGE IN EARNING CAPACITY

A change in earning capacity is probably the single most important reason for a modification of child support. Do not confuse a change in earning capacity with a change in income. It is not uncommon for an ex-spouse to quit his job or take a lesser-paying job and request a downward adjustment in his child support payment. This ruse seldom works, however, because a lesser paying job does not necessarily indicate a decreased earning capacity.

Example:

In 1963, the court awarded $200.00 per month support to the wife. The husband is now restricted to a 2/3 work load because of the removal of a kidney in 1972. In the meantime, the wife had become a licensed registered nurse. The trial court modified the support payments from $200.00 to $100.00 per month because of this change of earning capacity.

Generally speaking, an increase in either parent's income is a factor to be considered in a motion to modify, but will not alone justify an increase in child support.

In determining a change in earning capacity, do not overlook a corresponding change in net worth. New bonus or incentive plans, a possible inheritance, stock dividends, acquisitions, or other investments are all matters to look at that may have some bearing on your ability to obtain increased child support. Ways to obtain this information are covered in Chapters 5 and 6.

INFLATION AND THE INCREASED COSTS OF CHILDREN

Inflation and the increased costs of children are usually considered together. It is generally understood that the older children get, the greater the cost to raise them. If your current child support award is grossly out of line with the guidelines amount (discussed in chapter 2), inflation and the change in the age of your children can be a sufficient basis in and of itself to justify an increase in child support. However, if such an increase in costs was contemplated by the parties at the time of the divorce, then a request for an increase may be denied. The following two examples demonstrate how difficult the determination can be.

Example 1:

Wife was awarded child support in 1970. In 1972, she moved for increased child support based on the increased costs of raising the children and the husband's increased earning power. The motion was denied. In 1974, the wife again requested more child support, again based on the increased costs due to inflation, the advanced ages of the children, and the husband's increased financial worth. The trial court then awarded an additional $100.00 per month per child, based in part on the inflation that had occurred from 1970 to 1974.

Example 2:

Wife obtained child support in 1973 of $75.00. A year and a half later the mother moved to increase the support to $90.00 based on the increased cost of living, the increased cost of raising the children and an increase of $30.00 in the husband's income. The court denied the increase, stating that these factors must have been anticipated in the decree entered 17 months earlier.

REMARRIAGE OF A PARTY

Remarriage can have a dramatic effect on the amount needed for child support. If your ex-spouse has remarried and now has a higher standard of living, then this is an additional factor to be presented to the court in support of your motion for an increase. Conversely, he will argue that his expenses have increased as a result of his remarriage. Generally speaking, this argument does not carry much weight with the court; the prevailing attitude is that such additional expenses were voluntarily incurred by the ex-husband with full knowledge of his child support obligations.

DISABILITY OF A PARENT

If you have become disabled, or for health reasons are no longer able to work, you have a sufficient basis to increase your child support award.

CHANGE OF RESIDENCE

If you have moved to a new location, and this has resulted in a change in your standard of living, you may have a claim for increased child support. This is especially true if your children will be spending less time with their father because of the travel distance. The children will, therefore, be spending more time with you and your cost increases as a result. Also, you may have moved to a more expensive location than where you were previously and this can form the basis for an increase of child support as well.

ATTENDANCE AT COLLEGE

A different standard of support usually applies when a child attends college. If there is no provision for contribution for college in your decree, or if the expenses of college are greatly more than anticipated, you should consider a petition to modify to more accurately reflect the true state of affairs. However, courts will not usually require a parent to pay for an expensive school if they cannot afford it.

CALCULATING YOUR OWN CHANGE OF CIRCUMSTANCES

As is obvious from the above, the more changes you can show, the greater the possibility of an increase in child support. Ideally, you should show an increase in need and an increase in your ex-spouse's ability to pay. If one or the other of these is missing, your task is more onerous, but is not impossible. The following checklist will assist you in determining if you have an adequate basis for an increase of child support.

If, after completing this checklist, an upward amount is indicated, then answer the following questions.

- Do your children have the same standard of living (including the same luxuries and comforts) that they would have had if you were still married? Does your child support make up for this?

- Do the children work or do they plan to work? Are their earnings used for their expenses or for savings?

- What was your income at the time the child support order was entered and what is it now?

- What was the income of your ex-spouse at the time the child support order was entered and what is it now?

- Do your children have any special financial needs now that they did not have at the time the support order was awarded?

- What is the income of your current spouse or domestic associate, if any, and what is the income of the non-custodial parent's spouse or custodial associate?

- Have you or your ex-spouse acquired any significant assets through inheritance, investment, etc. that may have a bearing on your income level or that of your ex-spouse?

MODIFICATION CHECKLIST

COMPARATIVE INCOME AND EXPENSES

	Prior	Current	Net Change
Rent/House Payment			
Repair			
Insurance			
Taxes			
Water/Sewer			
Electricity/Gas			
Telephone			
Garbage			
Food and Household Supplies			
School Lunches/ Outside Meals			

Clothing	_____	_____	_____
Laundry/Cleaning	_____	_____	_____
Medical Insurance	_____	_____	_____
Medical Cost Not Covered	_____	_____	_____
Dental/Vision	_____	_____	_____
Drugs	_____	_____	_____
Car Payment	_____	_____	_____
Car Insurance	_____	_____	_____
Car Repair	_____	_____	_____
Bus	_____	_____	_____
Babysitter	_____	_____	_____
Child Care	_____	_____	_____
School and School Supplies	_____	_____	_____
Church	_____	_____	_____
Newspapers, Books and Magazines	_____	_____	_____
Barber and Beauty Shop	_____	_____	_____
Union Dues	_____	_____	_____
Retirement	_____	_____	_____
Payments to Others	_____	_____	_____
Children's Allowances	_____	_____	_____
Recreation	_____	_____	_____
Vacation	_____	_____	_____
Pets	_____	_____	_____
Gifts	_____	_____	_____
Extra School Activities	_____	_____	_____

Others: _____

_____

_____

TOTAL _____

TOTAL NET CHANGE, Earnings of Wife: _____

TOTAL NET CHANGE, Earnings of Husband: _____

TOTAL NET CHANGE: _____

TOTAL NET CHANGE OF EARNINGS: _____

TOTAL NET CHANGE OF EXPENSES: _____

TOTAL CHILD SUPPORT NECESSARY: _____

The results you obtain from using the checklist and the answers to the above questions are the identical issues that the court will consider in determining an increase in child support. It should also indicate to you the risk of any downward adjustment in child support that may be requested by your ex-husband. You should examine this information objectively and discuss it with other persons who can examine it objectively as well. If you have insufficient information in which to answer the above questions, you should utilize the discovery devices explained later in this book.

If an increase in child support is warranted, then it is time to take the next step.

FILING A PETITION TO MODIFY SUPPORT

The actual petition for modification that you file with the court is fairly simple. The example below is typical. It sets forth very simply the facts surrounding the current child support and concisely states the basis for an increase. Either you or your attorney sign the document and file it with the clerk of the court. The clerk will then set it for a hearing. You must arrange for a copy to be served on your ex-spouse; a copy must be served on him personally by either a private process server or by the sheriff. There is usually a fee of about $15.00 to do this. There is usually no fee to file the motion with the court.

SAMPLE 5: MOTION AND ORDER TO SHOW CAUSE, RE: MODIFICATION

IN THE CIRCUIT COURT OF THE STATE OF OREGON

FOR THE COUNTY OF MULTNOMAH

In the Matter of the Marriage of)
)
JANE DOE,   )   No. 5001
     Petitioner,   )
)   MOTION AND ORDER TO
     and   )   SHOW CAUSE RE: MODIFICATION
)   (Ex Parte)
JOHN DOE,   )
     Respondent.   )

TO: John Doe
               111 Main Street
               Portland, Oregon

          YOU ARE HEREBY ORDERED to file a written appearance by Affidavit in answer to the Motion and Affidavit filed by the Petitioner within thirty (30) days of the date of service of certified copies of this Motion and Order and Affidavit upon you, to SHOW CAUSE, if any there be:

          1. Why the Decree of Dissolution of Marriage entered in the above-entitled Court should not be modified to increase the amount of child support to the Uniform Guidelines amount.

          2. If this matter is contested, why judgment should not be entered in favor of Petitioner for Petitioner's reasonable attorney fees and court costs incurred in connection herewith pursuant to ORS 107.135.

          IT IS FURTHER ORDERED that should Petitioner fail to file such a written appearance by Affidavit within the time specified hereinabove, a Default Order shall be applied for by the moving party.

          DATED this _____ day of _____,
1993.

                                    _____
                                    CIRCUIT COURT JUDGE

IT IS SO MOVED:

_____
Richard W. Todd, OSB #79421
430 Pacific Building
520 S.W. Yamhill St.
Portland, OR 97204
(503) 243-2035

Motions to modify support are usually filed with the same court that handled your divorce or paternity action. The same case number is used that is on your divorce or paternity decree. If you are living in another state, however, you must normally arrange for a certified copy of your decree to be filed in the court of the county where you are now residing. You need to check with the clerk's office to determine if the copy needs to be certified and "authenticated" or transferred directly by the clerk's office of the court where you received the decree. Procedures differ in each state and the clerk in the county where you now reside will be able to tell you what is needed for their particular court.

Once the decree is entered in the court of the county where you reside, you will be issued a case number which will be used on all court documents that you file from that point forward, including your petition to increase support. File your motion to increase support and have your ex-spouse served. If welfare or any other public assistance is being granted to you or any of your children, you normally must serve the administrator of the agency that is providing such support with a copy.

The motion to modify should be accompanied by an affidavit from you which supports your position. The affidavit can be as detailed as you want it to be, but should contain, at a minimum, the information set forth on the example on page 44. It should be entitled "Affidavit in Support of Motion to Modify Support" and ideally will contain all of those things that you want the judge to consider in his decision.

SAMPLE 6: AFFIDAVIT IN SUPPORT OF MOTION AND ORDER TO MODIFY JUDGMENT

IN THE CIRCUIT COURT OF THE STATE OF OREGON
FOR THE COUNTY OF MULTNOMAH

In the Matter of the Marriage of:	)	
JANE DOE,	)	No. 5001
Petitioner,	)	
	)	AFFIDAVIT IN SUPPORT
and	)	OF MOTION AND ORDER
	)	TO MODIFY JUDGMENT
JOHN DOE,	)	
Respondent.	)	
STATE OF OREGON	)	ss.
County of Multnomah	)	

I, Jane Doe, being first duly sworn on oath, do hereby depose and say that:

1. I am the Petitioner in the above-entitled matter.

2. A substantial change in circumstances has occurred since the date of entry of the Decree dissolving the marriage of the parties. The changes in circumstances include, but are not limited to, the following:

(DETAIL CHANGES IN CIRCUMSTANCES AND RELIEF REQUESTED)

_____
Jane Doe

SUBSCRIBED AND SWORN to before me this _____ day of _____, 1993.

_____
NOTARY PUBLIC FOR OREGON   My Commission Expires:_____

To present information to the court that you feel is necessary will of course require you to have that information as well. It is therefore important that you request and/or subpoena from your ex-spouse or his attorney all of the information that you need to support your position. This is done through the "Request for Production of Documents", an example of which is set out on page 45 through 48 and discussed in greater detail in Chapter 8. Penalties or "sanctions" for failure to provide you with this information are also discussed in Chapter 8.

SAMPLE 7: REQUEST FOR PRODUCTION

IN THE CIRCUIT COURT OF THE STATE OF OREGON
FOR THE COUNTY OF MULTNOMAH

In the Matter of the Marriage of:	)	
	)	
JANE DOE,	)	No. 5001
Petitioner,	)	
	)	REQUEST FOR PRODUCTION
and	)	
	)	
JOHN DOE,	)	
Respondent.	)	

TO: John Doe, Petitioner

Pursuant to ORCP 43, Petitioner hereby requests that Respondent produce and permit the party making this request to inspect and copy all documents described in this request at the law offices of ___Richard W. Todd__, by __9__.m. on the __1__ day of ___July___, 1995.

As used in this request, the term "Documents" means and includes, without limitation, the following whether printed or recorded or reproduced by hand, and draft, duplicates, carbon copies, or any other copies thereof: agreements, communications, correspondence, telegrams, memoranda, summaries or records of telephone conversations, summaries or records of personal conversations or interviews, diaries, graphs, reports, notebooks, statements, plans, drawings, sketches, maps, photographs, contracts, licenses, ledgers, books of account, vouchers, bank checks, charge slips, credit memoranda, receipts, audit papers, working papers, statistical records, cost sheets, loan files, drafts, letters, any marginal comments appearing on any documents, and all other writings or papers similar to any of the foregoing, including information maintained on computer media.

Documents requested are all those in your possession, or in the possession of your attorneys, or under your control or available to you, specifically the following:

1. All federal and state income tax returns for the tax years _____ through ___1994___, inclusive, and documents showing any estimated taxes paid for tax years for which returns have not yet been filed, for you, together with copies of all partnership information returns prepared by or on behalf of any partnership to which you belonged during the same period.

2. All federal and state income tax returns for the tax years __1991__ through ___1994___, inclusive, filed by any closely held corporation, limited partnership or other entity in which you have, or had, an interest.

3. Any list of personal property prepared by either party.

4. All documents reflecting your income from all sources from _____ to date, including, but not limited to, W-2's, 1099's, wage statements and paycheck stubs

5. All documents showing any interest you have in real or personal property, including deeds, contracts, vehicle registrations, titles, bills of sale and any other documents concerning any assets in which you claim or may claim an interest.

6. All documents showing the existence and nature of any security interest in any asset owned by you or any asset in which you claim an interest, including, but not limited to, mortgages, trust deeds and security agreements.

7. All documents relating to the purchase of any real or personal property in which you have an interest, together with any closing statements prepared in connection with the purchase by you of any interest in real property.

8. All tax statements on any real property, business interest, or personal property owned by either party.

9. All financial statements prepared by or for you during the preceding five (5) years and loan applications submitted by you or any entity in which you have an interest to any bank or other lending institution or insurance company in connection with any application for a loan from _____ to date.

10. All documents evidencing your ownership or interest in any general partnership, limited partnership or closely held corporation in which you owned an interest at any time from _____ to the present, or in which you now own an interest, including any buy and sell agreements, stock purchase agreements and partnership agreements.

11. All documents which reflect the amount, location, and value of any stocks or bonds owned either jointly or individually by you.

12. All documents which reflect the amount and location of any checking accounts, savings accounts, money markets, stock brokerage or other financial institution accounts or similar accounts on which your name appears or has appeared, on which you are or were an authorized signer, or in which you have or had funds or securities on deposit, including periodic statements, cancelled checks, check registers (and/or stubs), deposit records, passbooks, and certificates of deposit for the period _____1993_____ to date.

13. Records of all charge accounts, credit accounts and lines of credit, including copies of all statements reflecting charges made and payments received on said accounts from the period _____1993 to date.

14. All policies of insurance on the life of either party, together with all records related thereto.

15. All receipts reflecting cash purchases by you from _____1993 to date.

16. List of all safe deposit boxes to which you have access, and a list of all of the contents of any such safe deposit boxes.

17. All records of all trusts, estates, life estates or other property in which you have any beneficial interest whatsoever, including a remainder interest or contingent remainder interest.

18. All appraisals prepared by anyone for any real or personal property in which either party has any interest.

19. Any and all stock option or stock benefits between you and your employer, and any information concerning receipt of such stock for the past five (5) years.

20. All documents concerning any pension, profit sharing, retirement, vacation, savings, PERS, IRA, SEP, KEOGH, 401K, Social Security, veteran's benefit, deferred compensation, or other similar plans, programs or accounts (past or present), including any and all statements reflecting your interest therein, any summary description of the plan, a copy of the plan, the name and address of the trustee, custodian and/or plan administrator or other officer in charge of each account or plan.

21. All records reflecting all income received by _____wife_____ (husband, wife, girlfriend, boyfriend) from all sources, from ___1993___ to date.

22. All records relating to any expenses or sums paid by you for which you have received reimbursement from your private practice, or your _____ association/employment with _____ .

23. All records of all trusts, estates, life estates, or any other property in which you have any beneficial interest whatsoever, including a remainder interest or a contingent remainder interest, including, but not limited, to any Last Will and Testament, Codicil or other instrument or bequest which names you as a beneficiary or contingent beneficiary.

24. Your current last Will and Testament, together with any codicils related thereto.

25. All stock certificates, bonds, indentures or any other security in which you claim an interest of any kind.

26. All health, medical, accident, hospital and dental insurance policies covering you or any member of your family.

27. All records reflecting any indebtedness that you owe, including, but not limited to, notes and contracts.

28. Any records reflecting any guarantee made by either party.

29. Any documents or correspondence concerning any credit extended by you or any debt owed to you by anyone.

30. All documents concerning any benefits available to you under any programs, Social Security, veteran's benefits or any other program, private

or public, under which you may have a claim for future payments of any kind or nature.

31. All documents listing, describing or showing the existence of personal property, jewelry, gold, silver, precious metals, gems, artwork, antiques, coins, stamp collections, or other similar assets in which you claim an interest.

32. Copies of all documents showing the existence of any lawsuit or claim against you or your spouse or by you or your spouse against any person or entity.

33. All documents showing any gifts, transfers or sales made by you of any asset with a value in excess of $500 during the preceding 36 months.

34. All documents showing the existence or describing any furniture, fixtures, office equipment or other similar assets owned by you.

35. All documents showing any farm implements, farm or logging equipment, tools or other equipment or machinery owned by you or in which you claim an interest.

36. All records showing any interest held by you in any livestock, horses, or any animal and all documentation showing the value thereof.

37. All documents showing any interest you have in any patent, trademark, copyright, royalty or other intangible asset.

38. All powers of attorney executed by you during the preceding three (3) years.

39. All documents of any kind or nature showing the existence or value of any asset of any kind or nature in which you claim any interest whatsoever.

****

This request is a continuing request. If the documents requested above come into the possession or control of you or your attorneys after the date requested for their production herein, Petitioner requests that they be produced at the time of their availability.

DATED this _____ day of _____, 1994.

_____
Richard W. Todd
Pacific Building
520 S.W. Yamhill St.
Portland, OR   97204   (503) 243-2035

After filing the Motion for Modification, the court will set a time for you and the absent father to appear in Court. It is common knowledge that people fear speaking in public even more so than they fear death itself. Speaking at a hearing and advocating your position can be a very stressful experience, leaving you confused, bewildered and exhausted. As a result, there will be things you will forget to say and important items of information that will be left out of your oral presentation. This is true for everyone, including attorneys. To avoid the omission of important information, you can submit your argument to the court in writing. Write down all of the information you wish to say and submit all of the information you want the court to consider prior to the hearing. The best way to present this is through the affidavit in support of your motion to modify the support. You can then tell the court at the time of the hearing as follows:

"Your Honor, if called upon to testify, I would testify to all those facts contained in my affidavit which has been filed with the court in support of my motion to increase child support. All of the information contained in that affidavit is the information with which I wish the court to rely in increasing the child support amount. If the court wishes to ask me questions regarding the information contained in my affidavit, I will be happy to answer them. Otherwise, I have no further information other than what is contained in my affidavit."

You can also write this statement down and just read it to the judge — no sense taking any chances.

The judge will take it from there. He may swear you in as a witness and ask you to affirm that all the information contained in the affidavit is true. He may have some questions that he wants to ask you. In any event, he will appreciate your efficiency in the use of judicial time while you, on the other hand, will have provided the court with all the information you want it to consider without fear of leaving anything out.

Your ex-spouse or his attorney will then be able to provide whatever information they want considered in objecting to an increase in child support or requesting a downward departure. Generally, their argument will fall into two categories:

1. They will dispute the information you have provided the court. If you have done your "discovery" through the request for production of documents, most of the information cannot be disputed. They will be left with disputing your expenditures, which they will claim are too high.

2. They will argue that the information you have provided is not a sufficient change in circumstances to warrant an increase in child support.

These issues are what the court is there to decide. If you have properly done your homework, and have carefully and objectively reviewed the information outlined in this chapter, then you should prevail and receive an increase in your child support award.

ALTERNATIVE METHODS FOR INCREASING CHILD SUPPORT

Many states have enacted "Child Support Guidelines" which were described in Chapter 2. Many states are also adopting an automatic review of child support awards to bring them into line with the suggested guidelines. In those states where this procedure is available, no change of circumstances need be shown. In most areas, this procedure currently is only available to persons who avail themselves of the child support agency to assist them. Otherwise, you must establish a substantial change in circumstances to justify the modification. If you do establish a change of circumstances, most states are increasingly setting the amount of child support pursuant to the child support guidelines.

Many people make agreements with their ex-husbands not to seek a modification of child support for whatever reason. In spite of any such agreement, you may still file a motion to modify if there has been a change of circumstances. You have a right to seek a review and the court has an obligation to examine the circumstances in light of the child's best interests.

LOCATING THE ABSENT PARENT (AND HIS MONEY)

ATTORNEYS
AND ATTORNEY FEES

WHEN DO YOU NEED THEM;
HOW MUCH SHOULD YOU PAY?

No book on the collection of child support would be complete without a discussion of attorneys and attorney fees. Virtually all people who attempt to collect child support use attorneys to some extent; unfortunately, over half the people who do so have strong complaints about the lawyers they hire. These statistical results are true whether the attorney hired was privately retained or worked for the government. Complaints about lawyers often occur as frequently as complaints about the absent parent themselves. It is essential that you understand what a lawyer can and will do; what a lawyer can't or won't do; and what a lawyer is unable to do in the pursuit of child support.

PRIVATE ATTORNEYS.

Virtually all books, articles, and general discussions give about the same advice for hiring an attorney:

1. Shop around and interview several lawyers who are specialists in the divorce area.
2. Ask about his professional associations and amount of experience in his areas of expertise.
3. Ask for references and talk to people who have used that attorney in the past.

4. Ask if they know what the law is on the areas you are interested in.

On its face, the above advice is logical and sound. In practice, however, all lawyers will be able to answer the above questions with assurance and confidence. Any lawyer who has been practicing any length of time will have no problem selling you on what a great job he or she will do. If there is any area in which lawyers as a group consistently excel, it is their ability to induce people to become their clients.

As a result, we have a situation where a majority of people are dissatisfied with the lawyers they hired to represent their interests. Most of these people find their lawyers through referrals from friends or family members. Some had simply picked a telephone number out of the yellow pages, made an appointment, and went from there. The reasons for the discontent are numerous:

- Failure to return telephone calls (the most frequent complaint)
- Failure to stay on top of the paperwork
- Failure to file papers in a timely fashion
- Not doing what they said they were going to do
- Not getting the results promised
- Being late
- Not informing the client of what to expect
- Charging too much money for the result obtained

In a recent study done in California, sixty women were polled on their experiences with lawyers and the legal system. Only seven of the sixty women voiced no vehement complaints about their legal experiences. Of those seven, three did their own divorces and three worked out agreements with their spouses before hiring attorneys. The seventh had entered law school upon her separation and completed her divorce with the help of a law school professor.

I can almost guarantee that you will never find a lawyer who is as concerned about your case as you want him or her to be. That type of attorney does not exist because no attorney can devote the exclusive time and attention to your case that you will be able to afford. The most you can realistically expect from your attorney in the collection of child support is that he fill out the forms within a reasonable period of time, take the other appropriate steps necessary to protect your interest, and keep you advised as to his progress in a timely fashion. He must also do this at reasonable cost to you and ideally collect his fees from the assets of the absent parent. If you can find a lawyer to do this, then you are miles ahead of most other people.

To get the kind of energy you want from your attorney, you must, in my opinion, hire someone that is relatively new to the practice of law. By new, I mean somebody who has been practicing law for only one to three years. This attorney must also be in practice by himself and not a member of a large law firm. He or she must have handled some domestic relations and collection matters, but it does not have to be extensive. It helps if that person's husband or wife is also an attorney and whose family is not totally dependent upon the earnings of the particular lawyer for financial survival. It really helps if the attorney is a woman.

This is cynical advice but realistic. Law firms generally must charge more money than sole practitioners because they have a larger overhead. They also usually have a policy regarding the amount of money they will charge on a case (their hourly rate) and the amount of money that must be paid in advance. This policy is to insure that some partner doesn't go "soft" on a client and erode the earnings of the other partners. It also insures a certain cash flow for the business as it can be predicted how the much the firm will earn based upon the hourly rate multiplied by the number of hours each attorney is expected to bill the client each month. If you can't pay the freight for this type of service, then you are dropped. Associates (attorneys who work for the partners) are generally newer lawyers, but they must also draw a hard line on billing you for their services in order to impress the partners and justify their continued employment.

Most sole practitioners and attorneys in small partnerships who have been practicing for a number of years will not be "hungry" for your child support collection business. Let's face it, collecting money from deadbeat fathers is not exactly the high-profile, sexy work glorified by TV shows and docu-dramas. It is hard, often frustrating work, difficult to do economically. The moral indignation the attorney experiences on your behalf is outweighed by past experience in this area, especially if the attorney has more attractive cases on which to work.

When you get right down to the nitty gritty, it is all a matter of money. You can hardly afford to spend $2.00 on an attorney to collect $1.00; you certainly cannot afford to pay $2.00 and receive nothing but frustration. Accordingly, you are limited in most cases to a relatively new, inexperienced attorney, a low-cost legal clinic, or a government lawyer.

The best way to find a young, inexperienced attorney is to call an old experienced attorney and ask him to refer you to one. Most attorneys will discuss a case with you over the phone and will happily refer you to a new attorney if you request it at the outset. If you have difficulty reaching an attorney on the telephone for a referral, ask members of the attorney's staff for a referral; chances are, they will know someone too. Younger, newer attorneys will try much harder to produce results for you on your case. They are interested in building a practice and you could be a good source of referrals in the future. As a result, they often times are willing to put in additional time at no extra cost in order to succeed. They are also more flexible regarding the terms of payment.

Try, if you can, to hire an attorney on a contingent fee basis. A contingent fee agreement is an agreement where the attorney receives a percentage of the amount of money he collects on your behalf. This percentage is generally twenty five percent (25%) to forty percent (40%) of the amounts collected. This percentage is negotiable and you should, in fact, negotiate it. In negotiating the contingent fee agreement, keep two things in mind:

1. The attorney in your case does not have to sue anyone to obtain a judgment. You already have a judgment; the attorney need only collect it. Because that work has already been done, the attorney should receive a lower percentage as the amount of work he must do is also lower.

2. You can normally collect attorney fees if you must take the absent parent to court (for example, a contempt hearing). Your contingent fee agreement must provide that the attorney fee amount is added to the amount you are seeking to collect. The percentage the attorney receives is based on that total amount. In other words, the attorney does not receive the attorney fee plus the percentage of the back-due child support. Alternatively, you could arrange for the attorney to not take a percentage of the back-due child support, but will keep all of the money awarded as attorney fees by the court for having to pursue collection against the absent parent.

If your attorney is unwilling to pursue your case on a contingent fee basis, then I suggest you try to locate another attorney who will. For some reason, some states prohibit contingent fee agreements on child support collection cases and this arrangement may not be available at all. If you find yourself in this situation, then you should next explore low-cost legal clinics for assistance. These clinics work on a reduced fee or sliding-scale basis (depending on your income) and are generally very good in the area of child support. Unfortunately, they are also in high demand. If they do take your case, their progress may not be as prompt as you would like.

Each state has a bar association that you can call for referrals of attorneys. You call the bar association, tell them the type of case that you need an attorney for, and supposedly you get the name of a couple of attorneys who specialize in that field. This can be misleading as there are usually no standards to determine whether or not a lawyer is a specialist in that field. A lawyer merely indicates that he wants a certain type of case and those cases will be referred to him or her. The bar association does not administer any tests to determine the qualifications of individual attorneys on the referral list.

There are other referral services that commonly advertise on television and in the newspaper that operate in a similar fashion. Lawyers who join this service are referred clients on a rotation basis, and pay a percentage of their fees collected to the referral service. The type of attorney you get can be a real crap shoot (literally).

Because of the thousands of lawyers available for hire, locating a suitable attorney should not be a problem. Paying the attorney fees to retain him will be a problem. Unless the attorney is willing to accept monthly payments, I would not even go in for a consultation. When you are calling around and discussing your case with lawyers, tell the attorney that you cannot afford to pay a retainer and that you must make payments on a monthly basis. The attorney can assess the likelihood of collecting the money from the absent parent and make a decision as to whether he will accept your case. If so, you need not worry about paying a large amount up front for legal fees.

There is no guarantee, of course, that you will be able to collect your legal fees from the absent parent. Although most states allow attorney fees for collection of delinquent child support, there is no assurance that the absent parent will pay it. It will probably be just as difficult to collect the legal fees as it is to collect the back child support, and the same steps must be taken to collect it. Recognize also that the amount of money the court awards you in attorney fees may be less—in some cases substantially less—than the amount of fees you actually incur. Numerous courts are very stingy about the award of attorney fees in these types of matters, especially those judges who haven't practiced law for a long time. You will have to pay the attorney fee you are actually charged, even it is more than what the judge orders the absent parent to pay.

Expect to pay $150.00 per hour for an attorney, unless you can retain either a low-cost legal clinic or a private attorney on a contingent fee basis. You should insist on an estimate of the total fees that will be required or, at a minimum, a range of what it is going to cost. Be aware also that you will be billed at this hourly rate every time you call the attorney or every time he opens his file. In addition, most attorneys will bill a minimum of 15 minutes for any work done on your case even if the phone call or letter only takes two or three minutes to complete.

In addition to the attorney fees, you will also be billed for any costs that are incurred on your behalf. These include photocopy charges, long distance telephone charges, fees for service of papers, and certain filing fees that must be paid as your case progresses. Make sure you get an estimate from the attorney as to what these costs are going to be so you can budget accordingly.

If you get a bad attorney, fire him or her as soon as possible. If you feel intimidated by the attorney and are unable to stand your ground, then write him a letter firing him and asking for return of your files. Even better, hire a new attorney and have that attorney fire your old attorney and represent you in getting your file. You should not, under any circumstances, keep an attorney that you are not comfortable with. You must keep in mind at all times that you are the client and he works for you. You have an absolute right to fire your attorney if he is not performing up to your expectations. It is not unusual to switch lawyers at any stage of the proceeding, and you should not feel uncomfortable doing so if you feel your attorney is not working in your best interests.

On the other hand, you should keep your relationship with your attorney on a professional level. Time is money for him as it is the billing of time that provides his livelihood. Too often, clients turn to the lawyer's shoulder to cry on and become incensed when they are charged for the time they use. If you must vent your anger or otherwise express your feelings, I suggest that you do it with a friend or relative. Use your attorney only to provide legal services for you.

GOVERNMENT ATTORNEYS

In Chapter 9, we will discuss how you can use the government to assist you in obtaining back child support. In order to avail yourself of the services of the government, you will in all likelihood work through a government attorney. These attorneys are commonly referred to as IV-D attorneys, so named because they work for the Title IV-D agency which establishes and enforces child support obligations primarily in welfare cases. However, you do not need to be receiving welfare in order to use the services of a IV-D attorney. In some states a local deputy district attorney is assigned to assist in the collection of past-due child support and they are often times referred to as "deputy district attorneys" or "DA's". All will be collectively referred to here as "government attorneys". All are provided by the government free of charge.

All states now have child support agencies that provide attorneys for child support issues. They can perform all of the services that a private attorney can perform and the maximum fee that can be charged to you to use them is $25.00. To apply, you need only fill out a IV-D application. If you are receiving benefits under the Aid to Families with Dependent Children (AFDC), you are required to cooperate with the government attorneys to collect support from the absent parent.

There are a lot of advantages in having a government attorney represent you in collecting back child support. The most important is that the services are free. In addition, they have access to a lot of information regarding the absent parent, and collecting from absent parents is all that they do. There are certain problems regarding the use of government attorneys, however, that you should keep in mind.

The first and most important thing to remember is that government attorneys work for the government. Most of the work that they do involves matters where the state has an interest or claim. People who use the government attorneys, however, feel that these attorneys are representing them and not the state; this may or may not be true. There have been numerous occasions where mothers receiving AFDC have told these government attorneys facts which indicate that the mothers have received overpayments. The attorney, after pursuing the child support claim, then reported the overpayments and became a witness in a subsequent collection action against the mother. There is also much concern about the government attorney's responsibility to seek full support payments and not to compromise the back child support arrearage which occurred prior to the mother's involvement with AFDC. After collecting the amount owed the state for arrearage, the government is inclined to cease any collection activity for any other amount that may be owed in back child support. Another potential conflict occurs when a government attorney pursues a non-custodial parent for support owed to more than one custodial parent. You could thus be in the position of sharing your attorney with someone else on the same case.

Perhaps the biggest problem with using a government attorney is that they have an overabundance of business. Currently, the government's ability to service child support collection problems, particularly in non-AFDC cases, is limited. Delays in working on cases are widespread and few cases are handled as quickly as clients would prefer. Increased publicity about the availability of free government assistance for non-AFDC cases will only make matters worse. Many people who have contacted support enforcement offices discover that the process works much better on paper than it does in reality. Too often the government attempts to persuade you to retain private counsel, and complaints of rudeness and inaction are common. Persons sometimes have to wait up to a year to have a file opened so collection work can begin, and often times persons are told not to even bother to try to contact the government attorney by telephone.

However, the child support enforcement laws require that states have local enforcement offices and have wage withholding available in all support cases. The government attorneys are required to withhold wages whenever the absent parent is 30 days in arrears. The IV-D offices must also have available and utilize 1) state income tax refund intercepts (for states having an income tax); 2) federal income tax intercepts; 3) liens on the debtor's real and personal property; and 4) reports to credit agencies concerning arrearages. They must also set up administrative processes to establish and enforce support with periodic review processes.

With the above in mind, you can see that this free service can be useful but is not without drawbacks. Most people use the government because they have no other choice. Some can afford an attorney but do not want to risk spending their money with no guarantee of results. My suggestion is to make it a tool like any other of the tools you have available for enforcement. Many enforcement techniques can only be used by government attorneys and they should always be used for that purpose. For example, the tax refund intercept and the IRS collection procedure can only be done through the government attorneys. If you understand their limitations, it can be useful and not nearly as frustrating. Their usefulness is set out in greater detail in Chapter 9.

CHAPTER FIVE

HOW TO FIND
THE ABSENT PARENT

THE ART OF SKIP TRACING

To collect child support, you must find either the absent parent or his assets. After all, you cannot garnish his wages if you don't know where he works and you cannot seize his bank account if you don't know where he banks. When a parent relocates and fails to notify anyone of his new address, there is little you or a court can do to collect child support payments should they become delinquent - unless you find him or his money.

Unfortunately for you, absent parents have a constitutional right to be notified of legal actions against them with respect to paternity and child support. As a general rule, documents you file with the court must be delivered to the missing parent and courts are reluctant to take any action without such notice. In the event you are totally unable to locate your ex-spouse or boyfriend, there are alternative allowable methods of service. The most common procedure is "service by publication"; your motion or request is published in the legal notices section of your local newspaper. This procedure requires a court order. A sample motion and order for service by publication is set out on page 67.

As a general rule, however, you will not be able to locate the absent parent's assets unless you locate the absent parent. It is also just a heck of a lot easier to "work your magic" if you know where the parent is so that you can serve him with papers. If you can find the absent parent, you can unload your entire arsenal of techniques on him and greatly increase your chances of collection. This will become more obvious as you read the subsequent chapters in this book.

Basically, this chapter is about "skip tracing". You are seeking to locate a person who has skipped out on his debts and his whereabouts are unknown. This area is almost exclusively the province of collection agencies, private investigators and the government. There is no magic in skip tracing, however, and you can do every bit as good a job as a private investigator if you utilize all the informational tools available to you. What is mainly required is tenacity and organization. If necessary, a little bit of trickery doesn't hurt either.

This chapter is divided into two parts: investigation that can be undertaken by yourself, and investigation that the government is obligated to do for you. If you have no desire to perform your own investigation, then you can skip to the section on governmental investigation and proceed accordingly. Be aware, however, that the government will normally take from six to eight months to obtain the information you need and quite often it is even longer than that. It is therefore preferable to exhaust all the resources available to you first before going to the government for help.

SAMPLE 8: MOTION AND ORDER TO ALLOW SERVICE BY PUBLICATION

IN THE CIRCUIT COURT OF THE STATE OF OREGON
FOR MULTNOMAH COUNTY

In the Matter of the marriage of	)	
	)	No. 1555
JANE DOE,	)	
Petitioner,	)	
	)	
and	)	
	)	MOTION AND ORDER
JOHN DOE,	)	TO ALLOW SERVICE
Respondent	)	BY PUBLICATION

Jane Doe, petitioner in the above-captioned matter, by and through her attorney, Richard W. Todd, hereby moves the Court for an order allowing Service by Publication pursuant to ORCP 7.

This motion is based upon the attached affidavit which is incorporated herein by reference.

_____
RICHARD W. TODD
Attorney for Petitioner

ORDER

IT IS SO ORDERED.

DATED this _____ day of _____, 199_.

_____
CIRCUIT COURT JUDGE

PRIVATE INVESTIGATION

Another alternative to locate the absent parent is to hire a lawyer or a private investigator. A lawyer will merely hire a private investigator to perform this service so you will basically be hiring the private investigator through the lawyer. This is not altogether bad; a lawyer works more often with private investigators and knows which ones can produce the best results for a reasonable cost. However, regardless of whether you hire the investigator directly or through a lawyer, it will be expensive. Their fees range from $30.00 to $300.00 per hour, and most will be reluctant to estimate the number of hours it will take to locate the "skip".

If you decide to hire an investigator, observe the following points:

1. Set a ceiling as to the amount of money you are willing to spend. This includes the investigator's expenses, which are not going to be included in his hourly rate.
2. Get an agreement as to his hourly rate and require an accounting of his time and expenses.
3. Check his references and make sure that he specializes in skip tracing.
4. Have him describe for you the procedure he will follow to locate the missing parent. Does it make sense to you? Is it an efficient use of time? For example, most investigation can be done over the telephone, which is much more efficient than field investigation.
5. Require periodic written progress reports and agree on their frequency.
6. Put your agreement in writing, including the services he is to perform, the hourly rate, the estimated total cost, the agreement to provide periodic reports, and your right to terminate him at any time with a return of any unearned advances.

As with hiring lawyers, an investigator's services have to be cost effective. You cannot spend more money on a private investigator than you will collect from the absent parent. I suggest you try it yourself first.

I have arranged this chapter in order of degree of complexity. Unlike most other areas of your life, it is often the easiest steps in skip tracing that produce the quickest and best results and the following steps can be accomplished by virtually anyone.

THE BASICS

Other than the parent's name, the single most important item of information that you need is the absent parent's social security number. There are several places you can check to discover the social security number: tax returns, loan applications, insurance policies, medical records, and bank account and business statements. Some states use a person's social security number on their driver's license.

In addition, before you even get started, write down the following information; it will be invaluable in your subsequent investigative steps:

1. What is the absent parent's full name and nickname?
2. Does the absent parent use any other name?
3. What is the absent parent's date and place of birth?
4. List the names and addresses of his parents, including the maiden name of the absent parent's mother.
5. What is the absent parent's current address and phone number; if unknown, the last known address and phone number and the date when such information was current.
6. What was the absent parent's address and phone number prior to the last known address and phone number?
7. What is the absent parent's current employment, including the name and address of the company, the name of his supervisor and type of work done?
8. What is the absent parent's previous employment, including the name of the company, length of employment, name of supervisor, and type of work done.
9. List any remarriage of the absent parent, the identifying date and location of marriage, the spouse's maiden name and the spouse's place of employment.
10. List any real property owned by the absent parent.
11. List any private, military or government pension or ben-

efits received by the absent parent or expected to be received by him.

12. List the names, addresses and telephone numbers of the absent parent's friends and relatives.
13. List the hobbies of the absent parent.
14. List the clubs or organizations to which the absent parent belongs.
15. Identify any criminal conviction of the absent parent including the date and location of the conviction, the offense of which he was convicted and the date and location of any incarceration.
16. If the absent parent is on probation, list the county and state where the probation is supervised and the name of the probation officer.
17. Note any military service of the absent parent, identifying the branch of service, date and location of assignment, the absent parent's rank and service number.
18. Identify any creditors of the absent parent.
19. Identify the absent parent's drivers license number and any other ID information.
20. List the name, address and telephone number of the absent parent's insurance agent or former insurance agent, banker or former banker.

After assembling this information on a sheet, sit back and think of records that you may still have in your possession that could provide leads to his location. Assemble any educational records of his that you may have, old bank books and checking statements, postmarks on envelopes received from the absent parent, a possible expired passport, recent photographs, and most important, prior tax returns.

Copies of tax returns reveal bountiful information regarding identifying numbers and clues as to assets. It not only provides his social security number and a possible tax identification number, it also lists potential assets that you may have forgotten about. If you do not have a copy of your tax return, you can request one from the IRS.

TELEPHONE DIRECTORIES

I have even known private investigators who have neglected to look in the telephone book or call directory assistance to find a missing person. If the absent parent has a telephone with a published listing, the telephone book will provide his residential address and telephone number. If the absent parent has relocated since the telephone book was printed, the present resident may know whether the absent parent left a forwarding address or telephone number.

If you know or have an idea as to where the absent parent has moved, call directory information for that city and surrounding cities and ask if that person has a telephone number. Once again, if they do, you can also obtain their address. If the number is "unpublished at the customer's request", you know that the person is in that city and you can locate them in ways that will be discussed later.

Alternatively, you can go to the library and look through the telephone directories of likely cities where the absent parent may have relocated. Most public libraries have telephone directories going back several years for virtually every city in the country. If the absent parent has a telephone number or had one in the past, you should eventually be able to locate it. If the absent parent has a new wife or roommate, it is wise to check under her name as well, as frequently the absent parent will hide behind the name of his mate.

THE POST OFFICE

For three dollars the post office will provide you the forwarding address of the absent parent if he filed one. Forwarding addresses are kept on file at the post office where the person last received mail. If the absent person was using a post office box, you can get the street address used by the absent parent on the rental application form. If the post office box was used for business, the post office will give you the information over the phone.

The fastest way to obtain a forwarding address is to go to the branch of the post office where the absent parent formerly received mail. You must fill out a Freedom of Information request form (provided to you at the post office) and pay them three dollars. They will immediately check and provide you with any forwarding address they have on file. A copy of the Freedom of Information request form can be found on page 73.

You can also mail a Freedom of Information request form to the post office, but it can take up to a month to obtain a response. Alternatively, you can send a letter to the absent parent at his last known address with a notation on the envelope that states "address correction requested". The post office will forward the letter to the absent parent and send you a notice of the address change. This procedure may be unwise if you do not want the absent parent to know that you are looking for him.

You may discover that the absent parent has moved more than one time and, therefore, you must submit repeated Freedom of Information requests. If you want to know if the person is still at the address you have for him, you can add on the form "addressee has not moved" in a box for the postal clerk to initial. Send the form and a check for three dollars by mail to the postmaster at the address of the station where the address of the absent parent's address was last serviced. You can obtain the station's address by calling the main post office for that city and giving them the zip code of the absent parent's address. They will provide you the address and phone number of the station servicing that address. Each new address you obtain should be followed up with a similar request until you receive back a request that states that the absent parent has not moved.

SAMPLE 9: FREEDOM OF INFORMATION REQUEST

FREEDOM OF INFORMATION
(Non-Government Agency Request)

From	NAME (Print)	$3.00 fee received
	ADDRESS	by:Cash_____
	CITY, STATE, ZIP CODE	Check_____ Receipt
Postmaster:		Number_____ Station Round-Date

I request the new address of _____

formerly receiving mail at _____Portland, OR _____
                                                             ZIP CODE

Requested by _____
                              (Signature)

Date New Address Furnished _____

New Address   _____   by _____

Once again, it is wise to check on forwarding addresses for possible mates of the absent parent and possibly even relatives and friends to locate them for information.

CITY DIRECTORIES

City directories are always located at the local library or possibly the Chamber of Commerce. With the city directory, you can look up the phone number of the absent parent and it will show the address where he is located. You should also review the residence listing (arranged alphabetically) for the absent parent's address and phone number. Often times it will state that person's occupation and place of employment.

The city directory's phone listing is a good resource if the only information one has is the absent parent's phone number. It is primarily utilized to obtain an address for service of legal documents on the absent parent. It has many other uses which we will discuss in more detail in the section on Landlords, Neighbors and Other Acquaintances.

DEPARTMENT OF MOTOR VEHICLES

Information on file with the Department of Motor Vehicles (DMV) is a matter of public record. In virtually all states, the

Department will provide you with an address and a list of vehicles that are registered in the name of the absent parent. The fee is normally minimal. You will need to provide the Department the absent parent's full name and date of birth. The DMV is normally divided into a driver record division and a registration division. The driver division will have on file the address a person submitted in order to obtain a driver's license and will contain the person's driving record. If the absent parent has received a ticket, it may provide an address (often invalid). It can also indicate a location where the absent parent does a lot of driving. The registration division will have a residential address on file if the absent parent owns a motor vehicle. Checking with the two divisions may reveal two different addresses. It may also reveal the name of the insurance company insuring the vehicle; this is useful in locating assets.

The addresses you obtain from DMV can then be checked with the post office to determine if the person is residing there or has moved and left a forwarding address.

The addresses for the Department of Motor Vehicles for all states can be found at your local library.

VOTER REGISTRATION

Voter registration records, open to the public, list home addresses of the voter. They normally also contain the voter's occupation, date of birth and political party affiliation. Once again, you should also check the absent parent's new mate or other close relatives for future reference.

UTILITY COMPANIES

Local utility companies will occasionally provide information concerning the address, telephone number, and employment of a customer if you can dream up a good enough reason for them to give you this information. For some reason, many of them do not feel that child support enforcement is a good enough reason.

INSURANCE COMPANIES

Insurance coverage of any kind can lead to the absent parent. He may apply for medical insurance, worker's compensation insurance, health insurance, fire insurance, employment group insurance, bonding insurance, or disability insurance.

The first person to check with is the local insurance agent who handles your own insurance. He may be willing to check his sources to determine whether or not the absent parent has applied for any insurance. For example, if the absent parent has applied for life insurance, his insurance carrier will have an application with his address history, occupation, employer and other valuable data that can provide leads to not only him, but his assets as well.

Life insurance companies have the medical information bureau to protect themselves from fraudulently concealed medical conditions. There is also a casualty index, a fire underwriter's investigation bureau, and many other cross-references where the absent parent's name might turn up.

The individuals insurance identification number is normally his social security number. As a result, the central computer for the insurance company will store their information with this numbering system. A common tactic of private investigators is to contact the insurance company and identify themselves as the absent parent to "double check to see if you have my most recent address". Invariably the company will provide the investigator with the address in the file and the search is over.

BOSSES, LANDLORDS AND OTHER SOURCES

You can obtain the phone number of the neighbor of the absent parent's last address by looking up the addresses in the city directory discussed above. For example, if the absent parent formerly lived at 1220 Elm Street, you can look up 1218 Elm Street and 1222 Elm Street in the directory and call the next door neighbors. You would be surprised at the amount of information these next door neighbors have if approached in the right fashion:

You: Hello, is this Mrs. Smith?

Mrs. Smith: Yes

You: Mrs. Smith, your next door neighbor ordered some clothing (or whatever) from us and we shipped it to him at 1220 Elm Street. However, it was returned because he apparently has moved and we do not know his forwarding address. Do you happen to know where he has moved, or where he works, or have any idea how we can locate him or how we can contact him?

Once you get the ball rolling, you can obtain a surprising amount of information from these neighbors. If their response is to tell you that the person was a jerk, then come clean and tell them you are really trying to collect money from him and agree that he is a jerk. Either way, you should be able to obtain whatever information they have regarding their former neighbor.

Former landlords are also a good source of information as the absent parent will most likely have filled out a rental application and will most likely have left a forwarding address to receive their security deposit or other refund to which they may be entitled. If the person was evicted or skipped out owing rent, you will probably also get the landlord's cooperation with whatever information he has in return for your sharing the information with him. While you're at it, garnish his refund (See Chapter 7).

Previous employers are also a good source of information. Federal law requires employers who are withholding an absent parent's wages pursuant to Public Law 98-378 to promptly notify the state upon temination of employment and to provide the absent parent's last known address and name and address of the absent parent's new employer if known. This is seldom done, however, and can only be normally obtained through the government (discussed later in this chapter).

If the employer you are talking to thinks you are looking for the person to collect back child support, they are often unwilling to provide any information. It is far preferable to use the "unable to deliver merchandise" subterfuge. You might also call the employer or former employer. Say you are an apartment manager and have a rental application filled out by the absent parent and you are calling to verify his employment. If his employment is confirmed, you have hit pay dirt.

If the former employer is cooperative, try to find out what address the absent parent's W-2 form was mailed to. You can also call the friends and relatives of the absent parent and try to obtain information from them. Recognize, however, that they are often more suspicious than the neighbors, more reluctant to give out any information, and will no doubt tell the absent parent about the inquiry.

STATE AND LOCAL GOVERNMENT RECORDS

Corporation Files. The Secretary of State keeps records of corporations, limited partnerships and assumed business names. They will generally have the names and addresses of the officers of the corporations or the registered agents of these corporations. These records are open to the public and the information can usually be obtained over the telephone.

State Tax Boards/Unified Registration Agencies. These agencies collect income taxes, "B and O" taxes, sales taxes, etc. Any business involved in business activity within a state that requires a sales tax must apply with the state for a license. This information is often available to the public.

County Recorder. A county recorder will have property tax information on properties, records of all judgments, birth and death certificates, marriage certificates, possibly military discharges, possibly gun permits, and, in some states, assumed business names of all registered businesses in the county, together with their owner's name and addresses. If you examine a marriage application of the absent spouse, take note of the applicant's maiden names. Any old addresses should be noted as these may contain the addresses of parents who can be contacted on some subterfuge as discussed earlier.

City Business Licenses and Permits. In virtually all cities, any business must have a business license. At the city clerk's office, you can generally obtain a copy of any application for a city business license or permit. It will contain the name, address and telephone number of the owner or agent and other data. You can get a copy of the name of anyone applying for a permit, such as a vending permit, a dog license, a parking permit, fire permit, sign permit, bicycle license, etc. If the absent parent has moved to another city and is involved in a specialty type of business, the chances are that he will continue in that type of business in another city and may need a permit or license to do so.

Real Property Records. Usually filed with the county, real property records will show the land documents of buyers, sellers, financiers (including banks and mortgage companies), and properties that may be owned by the absent parent. If the property was sold on a contract, the new buyers will be able to tell you where they send the payments.

Personal Property Files. Personal property files contain the name and addresses of people who own personal property who must pay taxes on them.

Court Files. Court files contain records of lawsuits and are indexed by plaintiff (the person who files the lawsuit) and defendants (the person who gets sued). From these indexes you can find out if your absent parent has been sued or is suing anyone. Follow up on any information that you obtain. These files also contain records of divorce suits, probate and criminal actions and convictions. While you are at it, you may want to check the small claims court files for the same information. Check under both the absent parent's name and the name of any business he may operate under.

Criminal Records. Federal criminal files will contain information regarding criminal actions. Most of the helpful information is restricted, but it may provide the name of a parole or probation officer that you can contact to obtain more information. County criminal felony files are kept in the county of conviction. The file will contain a lot of information regarding the person's history and the sentence he received. Misdemeanor and felony files are both kept in the criminal court section of the courthouse at the clerk's office. The Highway Patrol may have vehicle accident reports with details of auto accidents involving the absent parent. If the absent parent is a poor driver or an alcoholic, he may have a history of traffic accidents which will have names of insurance companies, people involved, etc.

OCCUPATIONAL SOURCES

The absent parent may be engaged in an occupation where licensing is involved, such as insurance, real estate, medicine, etc. If the absent parent is engaged in such an occupation, the licensing bureau will disclose the addresses it has on file for that person. Trade unions can provide you with current addresses, and the Secretary of State's office will usually be able to check into any licenses obtained by the absent parent in that state.

If the absent parent works for a union (such as a plumber), you should contact the state trade union. If the absent parent has moved out of state, the national union office may have a current address or place of employment. If the absent parent has a trade or business, he may belong to an association representing that trade or business and they may be able to help you in locating him. If your absent parent is a trucker or in the transportation business, he will need a license from the Interstate Commerce Commission who will provide you with this public information. If involved in any type of telephone, computer, or communication business, he will need to be licensed with the Federal Communication Commission. If he is a pilot, whether amateur or professional, he will need a license regulated by the Federal Aviation Administration.

You must sit back and carefully think of every possible area that the person might touch in the conduct of his business. If you know the type of work that he performs, you can contact other people in that field for leads. For example, if the person is a carpenter, you should check local construction supply companies; these companies often have lists of names and phone numbers of local contractors.

HOBBIES

One should always check fishing and hunting licenses if the absent parent is involved in any way in that avocation. In many states these records are centralized and are always open to the public.

If the absent parent has an unusual hobby which requires a specialized store, a conversation with the store owners will often bear fruit. We once located an absent parent because of his fetish for tropical fish. The store owner was most helpful with providing information regarding this particularly obnoxious customer.

SCHOOLS AND ALUMNI ASSOCIATIONS

Schools where the absent parent attended may have current addresses for the parent. They also may be able to provide a date of birth and a social security number if you haven't already obtained that information. Alumni associations may have a current address on the absent parent as well as any fraternity alumni associations who normally keep close tabs on their former "brothers" for future contributions.

FRATERNAL ORGANIZATIONS

If the absent parent was a Mason, an Elk, a Moose, or a

Goose, he may reassociate with this fraternal organization at his new location.

MILITARY

Each military branch operates a world-wide locater service. Requests for this service should be in writing and should emphasize that the location of the military person is necessary for child support enforcement. You need to provide the absent parent's full name, social security number, or service number (if known), date of birth, rank, and the location and time period of the absent parent's last known duty assignment. There may be a small fee for use of this locater service, so call beforehand to find out the specific procedures.

The addresses and telephone numbers of the locater services are as follows:

United States Army
Commander U.S. Army Records and Evaluations Center
Fort Benjamin
Harrison, Indiana   46429-5301
(317) 542-4211

United States Air Force
USAF Personnel Center
Attn: World-Wide Locater
MPCD 0039504 I H 35
N. San Antonio, TX   78150
(512) 652-5774

United States Navy
Navy Military Personnel Command
Navy Annex
Washington, D.C.   20370
(202) 694-3155

United States Marine Corps
Commandant of the Marine Corps
Code MMRB-10
Attn: Locater Service
Washington, D.C. 20380-0001
(202) 694-1624 or (202) 694-2436

United States Coast Guard
Commandant United States Coast Guard
Coast Guard Locater Service
GPE3-45 (If enlisted personnel)
GPO2-42 (If officer)
2100 Second Street S.W.
Washington, D.C. 20593
(202) 426-8898

Merchant Marine
U.S. Coast Guard
2100 Second Street S.W.
Washington, D.C. 20590

Always write to the Army first if you do not know what branch of service to which the person is attached. Since the Army is numerically larger than any other branch, that is the logical place to start.

CREDIT BUREAU INFORMATION

Credit reports are a great source of information if you can get one. They provide information on the person's residence, employment, credit history, financial information and asset data. The only problem is with obtaining one as a private individual; disclosure of information in a credit report has numerous restrictions.

A credit report is obtained from a credit bureau which assembles consumer credit information for the purpose of fur-

nishing consumer reports to various businesses and lending institutions. To get a credit report, you must normally be a subscriber
to the credit bureau. Subscribers are normally only businesses
who extend credit or collection agencies. If such a subscriber can
obtain a credit report for you, it can be a shortcut both to finding
the absent parent and to locating potential assets. Once you
obtain the report, the credit bureau will assist you in interpreting
the report over the telephone.

A private individual cannot use credit reports solely for the
purpose of locating the absent parent. Government attorneys do,
however, have access to the information in a credit report pursuant to federal law. This law allows a credit bureau to provide a
governmental agency with address and employment information
contained on its credit records.

In order to obtain a credit report for an absent parent, there
must be an order of child support that the attorney is seeking to
enforce. In essence, you have become a judgment creditor and
are, therefore, entitled to disclosure of this information. Under
those circumstances, even a private attorney can have access to
credit bureau reports to enforce the child support order. This
right of a private attorney to obtain this information is not universally accepted and a government attorney has easier access to this
information. However, the Federal Trade Commission has inter-
preted federal law to mean that a private attorney seeking to collect child support pursuant to a valid court order qualifies for
credit report information under federal law.

PARENT LOCATOR SERVICES

Whether you are receiving governmental assistance or not,
both the federal and state governments provide "parent locater"
services free of charge. They not only have access to all of the
information we have discussed so far in this chapter, they can
check records of the absent parent that are normally untouchable
because of privacy laws. This includes, when necessary, Internal

Revenue Service records. The only requirement to use the parent locater service is the existence of a valid order requiring the payment of child support.

There is both a federal parent locater service and a state parent locater service. If the state locater service cannot locate the absent parent, then they inquire of the federal parent locater service to check as well. All location requests are done by government attorneys and are automatic when you are receiving welfare. Non-welfare parents or their private attorneys must go through a government attorney for location information. There is usually a fee for this service of approximately $10.00. The maximum fee that can be charged is $25.00 and that is for full services.

To access the locater service, you must go to your local state child support enforcement office and request a location search. You will complete a "registration of absent or putative parents" and pay the appropriate fee. You may be interviewed for additional information. The local support enforcement office will then enter the appropriate information onto their computer. The computer will automatically check police records, public records, and records of the Internal Revenue Service, the Social Security Administration and the Department of Defense.

Access to the social security records will also reveal the social security number of the absent parent. It will also provide information on whether or not the absent parent is located in a prison or correctional institution within that state. If the absent parent has filed a state tax return or received income in the state, most states have statutes providing for disclosure of that information to the government attorney. Generally speaking, all state and local governmental agencies must cooperate with this location service.

If it is learned that the absent parent is residing in a state other than the state in which you are located, the government attorney will contact the office of that second state. The state offices are required by federal law to cooperate with each other to locate an absent parent. If the state office cannot locate the absent parent, they will forward the location request to the federal parent locater service which will conduct a computer search of records of federal departments and agencies to obtain location information. The Internal Revenue Service will provide the home address listed on the absent parent's most recent 1040 tax return. The Social Security Administration will provide an employer address from an absent parent's last W-2 form. It will also check its beneficiary files to see if the absent parent is receiving social security benefits, and it will access the Selective Service, the Veteran's Administration, the Department of Defense and the National Personnel Records Center.

The state parent locater service must utilize all state sources of information; they must check the state records within 75 days of application. If the search is unsuccessful and must be forwarded to the federal parent locater service, the process time varies greatly. If the state locater service can provide a social security number to the federal locater service, the request can be accessed through the IRS and Social Security Administration within three to four weeks. If no social security number is available, the process takes a lot longer. Access is first made to the Social Security Administration which picks up a social security number in only about twenty percent of the cases it receives. The other eighty percent of the cases must be processed manually and they only have a fifty percent success rate.

It is not necessary for the state parent locater service to exhaust all of their resources before transferring it to the federal locater service. This is merely the custom and you can insist that the state parent locater service contact the federal agency for assistance at the time you complete the application. If the government is unable to locate the absent parent, they must automatically reinvestigate every three months for three years. In addition, after an unsuccessful search, they can request the IRS to provide access to information contained in any absent parent's 1099 tax forms. These tax forms are filed by banks and other financing institutions to report a person's income. They will identify earnings on investments such as stocks, interest on bank accounts, unemployment compensation, capital gains and other types of earnings. If any U.S. institution has filed a 1099 form on behalf of the absent parent, the IRS will match the social security number on that form with that of the absent parent. Approximately one month later, they will notify the local office that has submitted the request.

As you can see, it is very difficult for someone to avoid the information network that is available to you. Quite often, however, this procedure looks better on paper than in actual practice. In spite of the time requirements, the entire process can take from six to eight months, and sometimes up to a year. Surprisingly, caseworkers in local child support offices do not inform the custodial parent of these locater services, nor are these caseworkers aware of the types of records that can be accessed. Women who apply are often told that if they have a private attorney, they cannot apply for the locater services, although this is not the case.

If you run into a person who does not seem aware of the services I have described, then I suggest you give them a copy of this chapter rather than arguing with them. Addresses for all state child support enforcement offices and regional offices are listed in Appendix A.

CHAPTER SIX

FINDING THE ASSETS

HOW TO GET RESULTS

Most of you want to find the absent parent only to locate his assets. Quite frankly, most of you would rather find his assets than find the absent parent at all. You are, in fact, better off trying to find his assets without involving him in your investigation so as to avoid tipping him off as to your intentions.

As explained in greater detail in Chapter 8, you can require the absent parent to appear in court to tell you where his assets are. This procedure is not without its drawbacks, however, and you should consider at least two factors before dragging him into court. First, requiring him to appear in court will alert him to your effort to locate his assets. If you have any concern that he will dispose of his assets or transfer them in any way after notice of your enforcement efforts, you should consider locating the assets through other means.

The second related consideration is the value of the responses you will receive from him in court. Not surprisingly, many parents who are forced to answer questions regarding their assets give incomplete or misleading information, omit significant information, and are just plain untruthful. As a result, hidden assets will not come to your attention if you rely solely on his answers to your questions.

Because the transfer of assets and the lack of candor in response to questions about assets are so common, it is wise in every case to ascertain the extent of the absent parent's assets prior to a judgment debtor exam or similar proceeding. Only after exhausting other investigative tools to discover assets - and ideally after attaching them - should you seek information from the absent parent directly.

As in trying to locate the absent parent, you must be creative in your approach, and examine every possible source of income and every asset that may be available for recovery. Once you do locate an asset or other source of income, you can then determine whether it is worth pursuing further for collection purposes. What follows is a list of common assets and location sources that can assist you in organizing your approach, together with factors that you should consider in evaluating those assets for collection. Some necessarily require knowledge of the location of the absent parent; some do not. Some require the assistance of a private attorney and some can only be researched with the assistance of the government. They are not listed in any particular order, so focus first on the ones you feel are most applicable to your own situation.

CREDIT BUREAU

Running a credit check on the absent parent is the best way to start your investigation. It preserves the element of surprise because he doesn't know you are running the credit check and isn't tipped off to hide his assets. It also avoids the stress of a face-to-face examination and can save you quite a bit of time.

The best way to get a credit report is through a private attorney. As explained in Chapter 5, they are generally only available to subscribers of the credit reporting service - either individuals or businesses who extend credit, or individuals or businesses who deal with collection. You will need to call around to various attorney's offices to find one who subscribes to a credit-reporting agency. There will be a fee for this service and it may require your assigning the claim for back child support to the attorney, at least for a short period of time.

The credit report does not necessarily tell you what assets the absent parent owns. Rather, it will provide you with his current and past employers, if any; his home address and prior addresses; the names of businesses or individuals where he has received credit and his payment record; any other judgments that he has against him; and the names of other businesses who have run credit checks on him in the past.

The value of this information is obvious. First of all you can find out if he has purchased the home where he is living. You can then drive by his house and see if there are any cars parked by his house, or boats or other assets. You can check his employment for a possible garnishment of his wages. If there is no current employer, the last known employer may provide you with information as to where he went.

If the credit report reveals the names of businesses where he has applied for credit, they should be contacted as well. Chances are that he has filled out a credit application which will reveal where he banks, together with other references. If the business will not voluntarily give you this information, you need merely follow the subpoena procedure explained in Chapter 8. These applications for credit will normally provide you with the name of his employer, his bank, and any other assets that he may have which shows credit worthiness. Such applications for credit can be a blueprint for your collection efforts.

If the credit report contains information about a Visa or Mastercard account, it will generally indicate some information as to the bank where it was obtained. Normally, the bank where he obtained his Visa card is also the bank where he keeps his checking account. That account can be garnished as explained in Chapter 7. Recent inquiries on the credit report from other businesses or other individuals are helpful too. Usually, these inquiries are based on an application for credit of some type and that information can be subpoenaed also. These inquiries are conveniently dated so that you don't waste your time on accounts that are "stale".

THE EMPLOYER

Certainly the easiest way to obtain financial information is through the absent parent's employer. If you know where the employer is, you can obviously garnish his wages, but other information can be obtained as well. Among the information that can be obtained is the following:

- any bonuses received or expected to be received;
- information regarding pensions or other retirement plans;
- savings plans or payroll deductions;
- bank location.

The back of the absent parent's paycheck after it has been cashed will provide you with bank numbers and bank names that can lead you to hidden checking or savings accounts.

Employers are usually cooperative in matters involving the collection of back child support. Usually, however, they will only provide you with basic information and to get more details you will need to use the subpoena. If the person is no longer working for that particular employer, you should subpoena their records anyway because of the wealth of information it can provide. Just because a person changes jobs does not necessarily mean he changes his bank accounts, IRA accounts, or other places where he has a history of depositing money. Cancelled paychecks and other information the employer has can lead you to these assets.

TRADE UNION

If the absent parent is or ever was a member of a trade union, their information can disclose other employee benefits that the absent parent receives, such as bonuses, or union benefits.

Copies of any cancelled checks written to the absent parent can, once again, reveal important banking information.

TRADE LICENSES

If the absent parent is engaged in any type of profession which requires a license, the records of the governmental agency that issues the license should be examined. In addition to basic information regarding the operation of the absent parent's business, valuable information may often times be obtained from the bonds that are required for the license. This will, in turn, lead you to the bonding agency and the application used by the absent parent to get the bond.

The actual license itself may be an asset that you can attach and seize. Although this license is normally nontransferable, attachment (or even the threat of attachment) can affect the absent parent's business operation. If the absent parent wants to keep his business going, this will certainly encourage him to eliminate his child support problem.

BANK ACCOUNTS

If you know the bank that is used by the absent parent, you can subpoena that bank for account information, including cancelled checks and monthly bank statements. If the absent parent has a bank credit card, information can be subpoenaed regarding his applications as well. Information that you want would include interest income reported by the bank to the Internal Revenue Service on IRS Form 1099.

This bank information will also reveal joint bank accounts with other individuals who have access to the account. States vary on the procedure for garnishing monies in a joint account, but that possibility should certainly be explored.

Federal law allows government attorneys to request the IRS to disclose information on the absent parent's tax return relating to any interest income reported by the banks on behalf of the parent.

To do this, the government attorney must know the social security number of the absent parent and must have previously requested address information from the IRS which was not successful. The federal office of the Child Support Enforcement Agency forwards these 1099 search requests to the IRS every three months. If any U.S. bank has filed a 1099 form on behalf of the absent parent, it will be matched with the social security number on the form. If such a match is obtained, it will provide the name of the financial institution where the absent parent has his bank account, the bank's address, and the absent parent's account number. It will also list the source of the unearned income and the amount of unearned income. There is no fee for this service. Check with your local support enforcement office (see Appendix A).

CERTIFICATES OF DEPOSIT

If you suspect that the absent parent has a certificate of deposit, you should attempt to ascertain the name of the institution which issued the certificate. A government attorney can obtain this information for you by submitting a 1099 search request to the federal office of Child Support Enforcement. If interest has been earned on this certificate, the IRS can locate this information in the same fashion as described above in the section on bank accounts. Once the institution is known, you can subpoena it to obtain the interest rate, amount, and the maturity date of the certificate. You then have the enviable choice of garnishing the interest income on the certificate or executing on the certificate itself.

SHARES OF STOCK

If the absent parent trades on the stock market, or has traded in the past, this potential source of income should not be overlooked. For publicly-traded stock, you need to subpoena information from the absent parent's stockbroker or former stockbroker. This will provide you with information regarding his current stock portfolio and his history of trading activity. Any dividends he is receiving can be garnished; any stock he currently owns can be executed upon. Information on where he banks is usually evident in his file on trading activity. The absent parent may also own stock in the business where he is employed. Such information is readily available from the employer as discussed previously. If you feel that he has possible interests in other small or closely-held corporations, contact the Corporation Commissioner to obtain the name of the registered agent for that company. You can then subpoena the information from the registered agent regarding the absent parent's ownership interest.

Government attorneys can also obtain information about stock dividends from the absent parent's income tax return. A government attorney has access to this information pursuant to federal law and also through the 1099 project with the IRS. This is discussed in more detail in Chapter 9.

REAL PROPERTY

Ownership of real property is always recorded in the county deed records of the county where the property is located. The office where these deeds are recorded exists in every county in every state and are indexed by the name of the person who sold the property (grantor) and the name of the person who bought the property (grantee). By searching these grantor and grantee indexes at the recorder's office, you can locate any recorded deed that conveys property in that county to the absent parent. The registrar (clerk) will then assist you in locating the deed. The deed will provide the parties involved, a legal description of the property, and usually the purchase price.

If your absent parent's name comes up on either the grantee or the grantor index, your next step is to contact a local title insurance company and request a "lot block report". These reports are free and will give you up-to-date information on the piece of property that you are interested in. All the title company needs to obtain a lot block report is the legal description for the property or even just an address. This report will tell you who the current registered owners are and basic information regarding the property.

If the absent parent is the owner of real property, you can proceed against the property as outlined in Chapter 7. If the absent parent has sold the property to someone else, you need to identify where the proceeds of the sale have gone. For example, the absent parent may have sold the property on a contract and is receiving monthly payments which you can garnish. Alternatively, the sale proceeds may have been deposited in a bank or reinvested in some other asset. A subpoena to the buyers can hopefully provide you with this information.

The absent parent may be renting the property to someone else. If so, these rental payments may be garnished. The tenant, or cancelled checks of the tenant, may also reveal other bank account information.

You should check all counties where the absent parent may own property and not just the county where he resides. You may also want to check the tax assessor's office for possible listings as well. Your credit report, if you have one, may indicate mortgage companies or other such types of creditors; a follow-up subpoena to them may result in the discovery of other real property too.

LAWSUITS

All county courthouses keep records of lawsuits that have been filed. Their indexes show the name of the person who filed the lawsuit and the people who were sued. If the absent parent has sued or has been sued, the file can be examined for possible asset information.

The file may reveal that the absent parent has received money or expects to receive money as a result of a judgment or a settlement of a lawsuit. Any monies he has received can be garnished; any monies he is expected to receive can be garnished or liened as well. Some states even allow a lien to be placed on a lawsuit before it is resolved and that possibility should certainly be explored.

At a minimum, you should contact the attorney opposing the absent parent for further information. These attorneys are generally very willing to provide you with information in return for any information you can provide them. Alternatively, they may suggest that you contact their clients who will be more than happy to provide you with information regarding their opponent.

If the absent parent has been divorced from someone else, the divorce file can be examined for information regarding assets. The decree for such a divorce is especially helpful in identifying those assets which are granted to the absent parent.

MOTOR VEHICLES

You should always check the records of the State Department of Motor Vehicles. They will provide you with information regarding the licensing of the absent parent and automobiles that are registered in his name. They will tell you the type of vehicle registered, the license plate number, and the vehicle identification number. With this information, you can consult the National Automobile Dealers Association's Used Car Guide ("The Blue Book") to get its estimated value.

Armed with this information, you can determine whether you want to seize the automobile as set out in Chapter 7. Information on the registration may also reveal the name of the secured party who loaned the money to the absent parent to purchase it. That information can be subpoenaed from the secured party which may lead to other assets listed on the financing application.

OTHER CRAFT

Aircraft are usually registered both with the Federal Aviation Administration in Oklahoma City, Oklahoma (telephone number

(405-954-3011) and also with the individual state. If you cannot find a registration, you should check to see if such aircraft has a county tax listing. Failing that, you should check with local companies that sell that type of aircraft. Surprisingly, the airplane business is a fairly small market and local air fields and area pilots are often times aware of other pilots in their area. If the absent parent is a pilot or has been one in the past, you should definitely explore this possibility.

Boats are registered either with the state or with the federal government depending on size and tonnage. If you suspect that your absent parent owns a large boat, check with the U.S. Coast Guard to see if any vessels are registered in his name. Alternatively, find out the telephone number of the State Marine Board and check with them to see if the absent parent owns any boats in that state. You can also check with other boat owners and marinas that provide storage and docking facilities.

OTHER PERSONAL PROPERTY

If the absent parent runs any kind of business, the inventory, office furniture, and other business equipment are subject to seizure. You need only have someone go into the place of business and make a mental list of the equipment there. If a particular company is a supplier for the absent parent, that supplier can be contacted and/or subpoenaed to provide information regarding the absent parent's company. If, for example, the absent parent has paid for a shipment of goods from that supplier, you can attach the goods to collect your child support. This usually always provides prompt payments. Alternatively, if your absent parent is supplying goods to another, the recipient of the supplied goods can be garnished for any payments due the absent parent. This also is guaranteed to produce results.

If there is a personal property tax levy in the county where the absent parent has his business, the records of this taxing authority should be consulted. If you know that the absent parent owns valuable property such as art, coin collections or antiques, an effort should be made to attach this property. Routine items of personal property such as furniture are generally not worth pursuing.

SECRETARY OF STATE AND OTHER GOVERNMENTAL AGENCIES

If the absent parent is doing business under another name or has incorporated his business, the Secretary of State's office will have information regarding that business. In some states, a check can be made under the absent parent's name to ascertain whether he is doing business under any other name or is an officer of any corporation. Information thus obtained can be followed up by contacting the registered agent for that corporation.

If you discover that your absent parent is a stockholder in a corporation, you need to explore further the possible value of that interest. Stock, even in a small corporation, can be seized and sold at a sheriff sale. Frequently, even the threat of doing so will produce the money necessary to satisfy the past due child support. If the absent parent is a partner, his interest in the partnership can be executed upon as well. You can even have a receiver appointed for his interest in the partnership to receive any proceeds that would normally go to him.

BENEFITS

If you suspect that the absent parent is receiving workers compensation benefits, you should contact the employer or the employer's insurance carrier to find the extent of benefits being paid. Information can then be obtained concerning the amount of benefits, where the benefits are being sent, and how long the benefits are expected to continue. In some states, these payments or a portion thereof can be garnished. Contact your local child support enforcement agency for more information about this possible source of income.

Unemployment compensation information can be obtained by local child support enforcement agencies pursuant to federal law. Unemployment insurance carriers and employment service offices are required to inform these attorneys whether an absent parent is receiving, has received, or is expected to receive unemployment compensation and the amount of any such compensation. You can subpoena this information yourself, but not all states allow you or private attorneys to garnish these unemployment benefits. Government attorneys, however, can have amounts withheld from unemployment in all states if they cannot agree with the absent parent to have specified amounts withheld. Government attorneys can also request information from the Social Security Administration regarding any social security benefits that are being paid to an absent parent. The Administration will disclose to the government any records they have on file regarding any benefits received or any benefits applied for.

If you suspect that your children may be entitled to social security benefits, you should go to the local Social Security Administration office and inquire.

MILITARY BENEFITS

Active duty pay and pension benefits are also subject to garnishment and should be investigated. See Chapter 11 which explores these special situations in greater detail.

VETERANS BENEFITS

Information can be obtained from the nearest regional office of the Veterans Administration. These payments are normally exempt from garnishment. However, if the absent parent is receiving retirement pay as well as veterans compensation, and he has waived part of his retirement pay (taxable) in order to receive the disability compensation (non-taxable), then that part of the payment, which is in lieu of the retired pay, is subject to garnishment. This, however, is subject to yet another exception: if the entitlement to disability compensation is greater than his entitlement to retired pay and the parent has waived all of his retired pay in favor of disability compensation, then none of the disability compensation is subject to garnishment. The only exception to this rule is where the veteran has voluntarily requested that a portion of his disability compensation be paid for child support. Advice: Go for it regardless — let them sort it out.

TRUST INCOME/INHERITANCE

Information regarding any income from a trust account can be obtained by subpoenaing the trustee of the trust. At a minimum, you should require that the trustee provide copies of the tax returns filed on behalf of the trust over the last several years, together with any quarterly or annual reports that have been prepared and a copy of the trust instrument itself. Any income from the trust can be garnished except in the case of a "spend-thrift" trust. Such trusts are designed to avoid creditors and some states do not allow invasion of those types of trusts to collect child support. If you find yourself in this situation, you should contact the local child support enforcement office for assistance.

If there is a possibility that the absent parent is a beneficiary under a particular person's will, you should write the county office that handles wills and probate and examine a copy of the will. If the person has died without a will, and the absent parent may be a beneficiary, it is wise to consult with a lawyer regarding possible inheritance and attachment of the absent parent's intestate share of the estate.

GOVERNMENT OFFICES

In addition to the governmental agencies discussed above, the following may sometimes lead to valuable information:

- Bankruptcy Court filings
- Secretary of State Uniform Commercial Code filings
- Public Utilities Commission
- Fish & Wildlife (Fishing Licenses, etc.)

LAST RESORT MEASURES

When all else fails, private investigators have been known to examine the contents of a person's trash. Once the trash is put out on the curb, it is public property and you can legally take the trash and examine it for information regarding potential assets.

Another common practice which is surprisingly effective is the phony phone survey. A person calls up your absent parent and asks them survey questions about such things as where they shop, where they bank, and conclude by asking for basic "background" information: age, income, place of employment, and other information. The key to success is to bury the key questions - "Where do you bank?" - amongst a host of innocent questions such as where you buy groceries, where you do your laundry, etc. The other key element is not to get greedy; you only need a few nuggets of information to be successful.

COLLECTING
THE MONEY

CHAPTER SEVEN

ENFORCEMENT:
BASIC COLLECTION TECHNIQUES

GARNISHMENT, EXECUTION AND
WAGE WITHHOLDING

A s most of you are aware, a support order carries no guarantees that you will receive any money from the absent parent. The support order is only the first step in the collection process. The hard part is to enforce the rights the support order gives you.

As stated in the Introduction to this book, the phrase, "The squeaky wheel gets the grease" is the axiom of successful support enforcement. It must be more difficult to avoid you than it is to pay you. If you can force the absent parent into this situation, you will rarely fail to collect money from him. The only exception I have seen to this rule is where the absent parent's hatred is so deep that he is, in a sense, mentally ill. The type of person who would actually prefer jail to paying child support should probably be avoided and your energy channeled toward terminating his parental rights. The overwhelming majority of absent parents are not like this, however; they just plain don't want to pay you any money. Forcing them to pay money in spite of their unwillingness to do so is what the rest of this book is about.

Unless you can enforce your child support order, it is useless. Enforcing your support order basically means that you will be taking things of value from the absent parent and applying those things to the outstanding amount that he owes you. If he has cash, you take his cash; if he has a job, you take his wages; if he has a car, you take his car; if he has a house, you take his house. Implementation of these techniques is guaranteed to both greatly inconvenience him and persuade him to pay you on a regular basis to avoid you doing this again in the future. Leaving one's house for work in the morning and finding one's car has disappeared can really ruin your day, especially if you also discover that all the money has been taken out of your bank account as well. Such enforcement techniques will lead him to conclude that it is easier to pay you on a regular basis than it is to try to avoid you.

Utilizing the collection techniques in this book have the unavoidable result of educating your absent spouse or boyfriend to these techniques as well. Seldom will an absent parent leave a lot of money in his checking account again after you have garnished it to collect back child support. He will only do so if he has worked out some type of arrangement with you before. Similarly, rarely will an absent parent leave a car registered in his name after you have had the sheriff seize his car. Commonly, they will place the car in the name of a business or new wife or girlfriend under the misimpression that you can't take it under those circumstances. This problem will be discussed in more detail later in this chapter.

Unfortunately for these absent parents, and fortunately for you, these strategies of hiding assets under someone else's name, switching jobs and banks to avoid you, and similar amateurish efforts make the absent parent's life more complicated and more of a hassle. Continued efforts by you to collect money owed you becomes a battle of wills. If you persevere, you will eventually succeed.

Read the entire balance of this book before deciding on which enforcement techniques you are going to use. Keep in mind, however, that you are not limited to any one particular option, but can exercise numerous collection efforts simultaneously. For example, you can withhold his wages, seize the contents of his bank account, and take his car all at the same time. Not only will this maximize the amount of money available to you to apply to any outstanding support obligation, it will also further the goal of making it more difficult to avoid you than it is to deal with you.

The balance of this chapter is devoted to basic enforcement techniques that are most common throughout the country. Subsequent chapters are devoted to special types of collection or special types of problems that you may encounter. Remember that all of these alternatives are available to you with or without an attorney, but vary in degree of difficulty; they are listed by degree of difficulty, with the easiest procedures first. It is urged that you try the easiest methods first because they are generally the cheapest as well in terms of fees necessary to utilize them.

THE BASICS

The obvious goal of collection is to obtain payment. The easiest way to obtain involuntary payment is to take the absent parent's cash. The second easiest way is to obtain the absent parent's personal property and convert it to cash. The third easiest way is to obtain the absent parent's real estate and either wait for him to sell it and receive your share of the cash, or force the sale of the property so that you can receive your share of the cash. The hardest way to collect is to take cash or property in someone's name other than the absent parent and convert it to cash for you to apply to outstanding child support.

The way cash is obtained is through what is called a "writ of garnishment". Personal property is obtained through a writ of garnishment when the property is in the hands of someone other than the absent parent, and through a "writ of execution" when it is in the hands of an absent parent. Real estate is converted to cash through the filing of a lien on the real estate and the subsequent foreclosure of that lien by forcing the sale of the property. Seizing the assets of an absent parent when those assets are in someone else's name requires the filing of a "creditor's bill".

Each of these techniques will be discussed shortly. Before doing so, it is important to mention that some things your absent parent possesses cannot be taken from him under any of the above-described methods. They are considered exempt from enforcement and collection because the government has deemed these items to be vital to one's ability to exist in our society. Thus, for example, furniture up to a value of $1,200 is generally considered exempt from enforcement, as is one rifle (up to $500), tools ($750 maximum), books ($750 maximum), and certain benefits. These exemptions vary to a certain extent in every state but are generally quite similar to the exemptions provided to people when they file bankruptcy.

It is important to keep these exemptions in mind when analyzing the absent parent's assets for collection. If he has a car that is worth $1,500, it is not worth it to seize it. If the sheriff sells it, the first $1,200 would go to the absent parent, leaving you with only $300 which will be eaten up by the costs of sale. A similar problem occurs in the forced sale of real estate. The absent parent will have an exemption of generally around $12,000 to $15,000. Only if his equity in the property (the net he would receive after the mortgage, closing costs, etc.) greatly exceeds his exemption would you be justified in forcing the sale of the property because of the cost of utilizing this procedure.

Similarly, you cannot seize all of his wages. You can generally only take part of his wages; commonly, it is twenty-five to fifty percent of his net take-home pay. This reinforces the notion that one should exercise several collection techniques at once to assemble as much cash as possible. This also increases the "hassle factor" by making it more difficult for him.

In addition to the items that are exempt, there is the other problem of cost effectiveness and what I will call practical impossibility. Some things are not worth going after because of the expense of going after them and the reluctance of the sheriff to assist you. For example, assume that you have located the absent parent in another part of town and he is living in a house that you know is full of furniture, a computer, a big-screen TV, and a nice stereo. Outside the house is parked a beat-up car worth very little and you have been unable to locate any other assets of any value.

What better way to get his attention and collect the money owed you than to have the sheriff go into his house, take everything out, and sell it at an auction. Easy to understand in concept, and as attractive to contemplate as it might be, it is virtually impossible to carry out such a technique in practice. Although you have the legal right to do this, the sheriff's office is very reluctant to undertake such a drastic action. They may require collection fees and bonds which are too costly for most people to provide. Absent that, they will just flat refuse to do it, citing the danger and possible violence that could result when you come in with a moving van to take all of the absent parent's belongings.

Accordingly, you must be somewhat choosy in the items you wish to seize. Consider both the costs of seizure, and the trouble you and the sheriff must undergo to seize them.

SEIZING CASH OR ITS EQUIVALENT

As already discussed, cash or its equivalent is the easiest commodity to seize because you don't have to sell it. If you can locate the cash, it is relatively easy to take it so long as it is in the hands of the third party. Cash in the hands of the absent parent is normally obtained through direct order of the court at either a judgment debtor exam or a contempt hearing. These procedures are spelled out more fully in Chapter 8. Most people do not keep cash in their possession, however, but deposit it in banks or other financial institutions. Or, they are awaiting the receipt of cash, usually from their employer. Your job, therefore, is to go to these places where their cash is kept and take it. This is done with the writ of garnishment.

A writ of garnishment, as explained in the beginning of this chapter, is an order from the court directed to the bank, the employer, or other person who is holding funds for the absent parent, which instructs those third parties (called the "garnishee") to pay the money they hold for the absent parent into the court. It is generally a preprinted form that you fill out and take to the court for issuance by the clerk. It contains very specific instructions on what the garnishee should do. If the third party you garnish does not have any of the absent parent's money, they must so state in writing and file it with the court. You, of course, have the opportunity to review anything that is filed with the court and you will receive the proceeds that are deposited with the court.

A sample writ of garnishment issued to a bank is set out on page 109. You fill out all the information on the form and deliver it to the clerk's office together with a fee, generally three to five dollars. The clerk's office will check it for accuracy and stamp it with the clerk's seal. They will then notify you and you can pick it up to have it served, either by the sheriff or a private process server.

When the bank or other financing institution receives the writ of garnishment, they will generally comply with it to the letter. They will remove all of the money from the absent parent's bank account or bank accounts and send it to the court. Any outstanding checks on that bank that have been written by the absent parent will, of course, bounce. If it is in a joint account with someone else, the money will still be removed. In other words, it is very effective.

It is also very common. Banks and other financing institutions are accustomed to receiving these writs of garnishment and many of the larger ones have departments especially designed to handle them. Some banks require a certain number of copies and

SAMPLE 10: WRIT OF GARNISHMENT

FORM No. 1194—WRIT OF GARNISHMENT—ISSUED BY ATTORNEY.

STEVENS-NESS LAW PUBLISHING CO., PORTLAND, OR. 97204

OT   THIS FORM IS FOR GARNISHMENTS ISSUED UNDER CH. 873 §§ 2 AND 4, OREGON LAWS 1987

In the.................................Court of the State of Oregon

For the County of ....

.... *Plaintiff*

vs.

.... *Defendant(s)*

Case No. ....

WRIT OF GARNISHMENT
ISSUED BY ATTORNEY

IN THE NAME OF THE STATE OF OREGON, TO: ....

You are now a Garnishee.

AS A GARNISHEE, YOU NEED TO KNOW THE FOLLOWING (the following information is to be filled in by the Creditor):

On ...., 19........, plaintiff/defendant (cross out one) ...., named above and called "Creditor," has obtained a judgment (a court order for the payment of money) against the plaintiff/defendant (cross out one).., named above and called "Debtor." The Debtor's Social Security Number or Employer Identification Number is .... (insert if known). The following amount is necessary to satisfy the Creditor's judgment:

+ *Judgment Debt*	$_____			$_____
+ *Prejudgment Interest*	$_____			$_____
+ *Attorney Fees*	$_____	*Total other from additional sheet*		
+ *Cost Bill*	$_____	(if used)		$_____
+ *Post-Judgment Interest*	$_____	+ *Past Writ Issuance Fees*	$_____	
+ *Delivery Fee for this Writ*	$_____	+ *Past Delivery Fees*	$_____	
+ *Sheriff's Fees other than*		+ *Transcript and Filing Fees*		
Delivery Fees	$_____	*for other counties*	$_____	
+ *Other (Explain. Attach additional*		= *Subtotal*		$_____
sheets if necessary.)	$_____	*LESS Payments Made*	($_____	)
....	$_____	= *TOTAL Amount Required to Satisfy*		
....	$_____	*in Full this Judgment*	$_____	

THE CLERK OF THE COURT HAS NOT CALCULATED ANY AMOUNTS ON THE WRIT AND IS NOT LIABLE FOR ERRORS MADE IN THE WRIT BY THE CREDITOR.

I certify that I have read the Writ of Garnishment; and to the best of my knowledge, information and belief, there is good ground to support it.

DATED ...., 19........

....
SIGNATURE OF CREDITOR'S ATTORNEY

....
CREDITOR'S ATTORNEY (TYPE OR PRINT)   BAR NO.

....
ADDRESS

....
CITY   STATE   ZIP   PHONE

Page 1—WRIT OF GARNISHMENT—ISSUED BY ATTORNEY.

a processing fee, and most states allow the imposition of such a fee in order to process your writ. Call the bank you intend to garnish in advance to find out their procedures to receive the writ and where it should be delivered. This is especially important if you do not know the branch of the bank where the absent parent has his account. Many banks will now check all the branches if you deliver the writ to the appropriate head office. Save yourself some time and frustration by calling in advance to find out the exact procedure.

Once you have talked to the bank, go to your local office supply store and request a bank garnishment form. After you have completed the form, take it to the clerk of the court and request that it be issued. Some clerks will issue it while you are standing there; other courts take one to two weeks for issuance. After it is issued, arrange for it to be served together with any necessary copies and any processing fee.

Writs generally must be answered within five days. If the bank fails to respond within the time period, you may request a court hearing to find out why. The court in its discretion can order them to pay and, in some situations, can levy a judgment against the garnishee for failure to pay the money into court or otherwise respond to the writ. If you are not satisfied with their response, you can also request a hearing to examine the garnishee as to the circumstances surrounding the absent parent. This type of problem, with banks in particular, is very uncommon. It is a common problem, however, in closely held businesses and other self-employment situations. This is discussed in more detail in the section on Creditor's Bills.

Once the clerk receives the money from the bank, they are generally required to hold onto it for a period of time, usually ten days. This gives the absent parent, or someone else who has a claim to the money, an opportunity to file an objection to your garnishment in court. If no objection is received, the money is then turned over to you. If an objection is received, the court schedules a hearing to straighten the matter out.

The two most common objections occur when the absent parent claims the funds are exempt, or when another person claims the funds belong to him or her. For example, in most states you are only allowed to take a portion of an absent parent's paycheck. If he has deposited that paycheck into a bank account, the bank will give you the entire amount. If he properly files a claim of exemption on the grounds that you are only entitled to a certain percentage of his paycheck, you may only get a portion of the amount you garnished. Similarly, if he has a joint account with a new wife or girlfriend, and she can prove that the money at the time was in fact hers, the judge can order the money returned to her.

In most states, you are required to send a copy of the writ of garnishment that you serve on the bank to the absent parent, together with a list of the exemptions he may claim. This list of exemptions is a preprinted form that is usually available at the office supply store as well. Usually it is a good idea to review the garnishment laws of your state so that you don't overlook anything. However, even if you do make an error, it is usually not critical. Objections to the garnishments are infrequent and most courts don't have much sympathy for absent parents who are delinquent on their child support.

Use the writ of garnishment as your initial enforcement technique. It is the easiest and cheapest way to collect money from your absent parent and it is guaranteed to grab his attention, even though the amount you receive is small. Since it is difficult to function in today's society without a bank account, his knowledge that you know how to interfere with the use of his bank account can be a very powerful tool. Sure, he can change banks. But you can find out the name of his new bank, and as long as you are out there, he will never feel comfortable putting money in a bank account again. That is, unless he has worked out a satisfactory arrangement with you.

WAGE WITHHOLDING ORDERS

A special type of writ of garnishment is the wage withholding order or "order withholding earnings". It is a document from the court that tells the absent parent's employer to take a certain amount of money out of every paycheck and either pay it to you directly or to the court, depending on the state the employer is in. It is both inexpensive and effective. Its drawback is that you only receive a portion of the absent parent's paycheck. Its benefit, however, is that it is a continuing order and requires the employer to take money out of future paychecks as well. Under federal law, states must permit a wage deduction order against anyone who is delinquent more than 30 days or who has missed three consecutive payments.

There has been some confusion between a wage garnishment and an order withholding earnings. Traditionally, a wage garnishment is used by many people who have judgments, only some of whom have these judgments for back child support. Identical to the bank garnishments, the employer is only required to pay into court the amount owed at the time the garnishment is served. It does not include future payments that will be due to the absent parent. Under the child support enforcement amendment of 1984, a new method was carved out to simplify matters, called variously the "order withholding earnings", "wage withholding", and "payroll deduction order". Under this new procedure, the amount that may be withheld from each paycheck is also increased. In general, sixty percent of the wages may be withheld, plus five percent for arrearages in excess of twelve weeks if the absent parent is not remarried and has no dependents. It decreases to fifty percent of net wages, plus five percent for arrearages that exceed twelve weeks if the absent parent has remarried and has dependents. The employer must forward payments to the court or local child support agency within ten days of each pay period, and they are liable for any amounts that they fail to withhold and pay.

All states now have laws for interstate wage withholding and your local child support enforcement office can do this task for you. If you choose not to use the local support enforcement office, you can obtain an order withholding earnings yourself. A sample form is set forth on page 114. Once prepared, this type of order is taken to the judge of the family court where you reside and delivered to his or her clerk. They will arrange for the order to be signed or instruct you on how to do so. You must arrange to have this order delivered to the employer.

Employers cannot fire or otherwise discipline an employee because of your order withholding earnings. They also are required to notify you or the court if the employee quits and provide you with the name of his new employer if they know it. If the absent parent objects to the order withholding earnings, a hearing must be requested. The only defense usually available is mistaken identity; otherwise, the withholding begins.

Income withholding orders do not just cover wages in the traditional sense. The definition of income is very broad and you should consider all kinds of income in your collection efforts, including the following:

- Pensions
- Profit Sharing Plans
- Unemployment Compensation
- Pension and Retirement Benefits
- Workers Compensation Benefits
- Social Security Benefits
- Accident Benefits
- Bonuses
- Commissions
- Rental or Interest Income
- Military, Administration, or Disability Benefits
- Death Benefits
- Public Trusts or Disability Insurance

SAMPLE 11:   EX PARTE ORDER TO WITHHOLD EARNINGS

IN THE CIRCUIT COURT OF THE STATE OF OREGON
FOR THE COUNTY OF MULTNOMAH

JANE DOE, Petitioner,	) No. 5001))
and	) EX PARTE ORDER) TO WITHHOLD EARNINGS
JOHN DOE, Respondent.	))

TO: Employer   John Doe
         Address   Social Security Number

Based upon Petitioner's Motion,
YOU ARE   DELINQUENT
HEREBY   AMOUNT OWED $5,000
ORDERED TO   CONTINUING MONTHLY
WITHHOLD &   SUPPORT
PAY OVER TO: PAYMENTS: $110.00

an amount equal to 25 percent (or the continuing monthly support payment amount, whichever is less) of the bene iciary's benefits for temporary total disability, temporary partial disability, or an amount equal to 25 percent of the beneficiary's benefits for permanent partial disability and permanent total disability due or becoming due for each month beneficiary becomes or is eligible for these benefits, whether the benefits are paid monthly or in a lump sum payment.

      The Department of Human Resources will inform you when there is no longer a current monthly support obligation.

      EVEN IF THERE IS MORE THAN ONE ORDER TO WITHHOLD, IN NO EVENT SHALL YOU WITHHOLD MORE THAN 25 PERCENT OF BENEFICIARY'S BENEFITS DUE OR BECOMING DUE FOR EACH MONTH BENEFICIARY BECOMES OR IS ELIGIBLE.

      THIS ORDER supersedes any order to withhold previously entered and shall continue in effect as long as there is current support owed or until further order of this Court.

DATED:_____   _____
                                    CIRCUIT COURT JUDGE

For information or assistance, contact: Central Operations Section
                                      Support Enforcement Division
                                      1495 Edgewater St. NW, Suite 290
                                      Salem, OR 97304
                                      Phone: (503) 373-7300

An order withholding earnings or a writ of garnishment should be obtained in every situation where the absent parent receives some kind of payment from someone else. If he has sold something and is receiving payments for it, you should garnish those payments. Err on the side of garnishing anything that he receives. Any interruption or interference that you can generate in his income stream will not only provide cash to you, but will maintain the overall strategy of forcing him to commence regular payments to you.

EXECUTION ON PERSONAL PROPERTY

Execution on personal property is usually only advisable after you have garnished all manner of cash or liquid proceeds belonging to the absent parent. Execution on personal property requires that you sell the personal property to convert it to cash. As a result, this type of collection is more complicated and more costly than the garnishment procedures. It is, however, quite effective in getting someone's attention and in showing the absent parent that you mean business.

Execution on personal property involves three steps:

1. Issuance of a writ of execution and instructions to the sheriff to pick up the property;
2. Seizure of the property by the sheriff and transfer to a storage facility;
3. Sale of the property seized by auction and application of the auction proceeds to the child support arrearages.

To get the ball rolling, you must request the clerk's office in the county where your support order is recorded to issue a writ of execution to the sheriff of the county where the personal property is located. A writ of execution, in other words, takes the place of the writ of garnishment and is similar in format. A sample writ of execution is set out on page 116. It takes about as long to get a writ of execution issued by the clerk's office as it does to get a writ of garnishment and the fee is about the same, generally three to five dollars.

SAMPLE 12: WRIT OF EXECUTION

FORM No. 149—EXECUTION—CIRCUIT, DISTRICT OR JUSTICE.   COPYRIGHT 1968   STEVENS-NESS LAW PUB. CO., PORTLAND, OR. 97204
OL

In the .... Court of the State of Oregon

For the County of ....

....
.... *Plaintiff*

vs.

....
.... *Defendant*

No..................................

EXECUTION

To .... *County, Oregon — Greetings:*

WHEREAS, on ....*, in the* .... *Court of* .... *County, Oregon,* ....
.... *recovered a judgment against* ....
....*for the following sum(s):*

which judgment, or a certified transcript thereof, was on ....*, 19.......*, duly docketed in the *judgment docket of the* .... *Court of* .... *County, Oregon, where it remains in force and unsatisfied in whole or in part;*

    THEREFORE, IN THE NAME OF THE STATE OF OREGON, you are commanded that out of the personal property of the said judgment debtor(s), †or if sufficient personal property cannot be found, then out of the real property belonging to said judgment debtor(s) on or after the date said judgment was docketed in your county,† excepting such as the law exempts, that you satisfy the amount of said judgment with interest and costs and disbursements that may have accrued, LESS the amount of $.................................... which has been paid on said judgment, and also the costs of this writ, and make due return of this writ within sixty days after you receive this writ.

    Witness my hand and the seal of this court on this .... *day of* ....*, 19........*

Judgment Debt . . . . . . $............................	
Interest	....
Attorney Fee	*Name and Title*
Cost Bill	
Additional Costs	*By* .... *Deputy*
Total . . . . $............................	
Payments Made . . . . . . $............................	
Balance Due . . . . $............................	*Issued at the request of:*
Accruing Costs . . . . $............................	
Disbursements	
Keeper's Fees	
Mileage	
Total . . . . $............................	

Delete wording between † symbols, if not applicable.

EXECUTION.

As you can see from examination of the writ, it basically tells the sheriff to seize items of personal property of the absent parent. It is your responsibility to provide to the sheriff a list of the personal property that you want the sheriff to seize. The list must be specific; the sheriff will not just take anything that he finds on the absent parent's property. If, for example, you want him to pick up an automobile, you must provide him with the year, make, model, serial number and vehicle identification number of the automobile, together with some type of proof that the vehicle does, in fact, belong to the absent parent. This is generally done by the use of sheriff's instructions, which are submitted to the sheriff along with the writ of execution and the applicable fees. A sample sheriff instruction is set out on page 119.

Although it is surprising to many, a substantial portion of the sheriff's resources are devoted to process serving and execution on property. They are usually quite willing to answer any questions you have about the proper procedure in the county where the personal property is located. It is advisable to always call the sheriff's office in advance and ask them for their particular procedures. Some sheriff's departments require you to provide a tow truck, but most have a contract with the local tow driver for these situations. If a moving van is necessary, this can be discussed with the sheriff as well. It all depends on the type of personal property you are seizing.

You must also identify where the property is located because the sheriff will not search for it. If the sheriff goes out to an address you provide, and the personal property is not there, he generally will not ask around as to where it is. Timing is critical, but the sheriff's department will work with you on this.

They also charge a fee for this service and require a bond in the event that they are faced with some liability for improper seizure. Some sheriff's offices can be quite unreasonable as to the amount of bond they require and in most states there is no set bond amount. Therefore, you can negotiate with the sheriff on the size of the bond and I suggest that you be conservative as to the value of the personal property when you are discussing this with him. As a general rule, expect a requirement of two and a half times the value of the personal property you are seizing. Thus, a car worth $5,000 will require a bond of $12,500. Your insurance agent can arrange to get a bond for you if you don't know how. The cost of a bond is one to three percent of the amount of the bond. In our car example, the bond premium would range from $120.00 to $360.00 (1% of $12,500 is $125.00).

If you cannot get a bond by yourself, an attorney can obtain one for you. Insurance companies provide attorneys with preprinted and preapproved bonds for up to $15,000. The premium for these types of bonds is three percent. Few attorneys are familiar with these preapproved bonds and you may have to shop around to find a lawyer who even knows what you are talking about.

The sheriff will also charge you a fee for this service, usually around $50.00. In addition, he will require the towing fees and storage fees for the personal property to be paid in advance.

By this time, you can probably understand the primary problem with seizing personal property - it is very expensive. Before you have even taken anything, you are out the fee for the writ of execution, the sheriff's fee, the premium for the bond, the towing charge, and the storage fees. Even though all of these costs are added onto the judgment you have against the absent parent, you are still required to pay these amounts up front. It is therefore important that you realistically assess the value of the property you are trying to recover and make sure it is worth it. It doesn't make any sense to lay out this kind of money and go to this much effort if the item you are seizing is not worth much more than the costs of taking it.

Sample 13: Sheriff's Instruction

IN THE CIRCUIT COURT OF THE STATE OF OREGON
FOR THE COUNTY OF MULTNOMAH

In the Matter of the Marriage of:	)	
JANE DOE,	)	No. 5001
	)	
Petitioner,	)	
	)	INSTRUCTIONS TO SHERIFF
and	)	(Multnomah County)
	)	
JOHN DOE,	)	
Respondent.	)	

TO THE SHERIFF OF MULTNOMAH COUNTY:

YOU ARE HEREBY INSTRUCTED to execute the enclosed Writ of Execution for the following described personal property of the defendant, to-wit:

> 1989 Toyota Pickup, Oregon License Plate No. QEC 144, VIN No. 122435789

by immediately proceeding to debtor's residence located at 1111 Anywhere Road, Portland, Oregon 55555, or to such other location as may be hereafter identified within your county and at such place or places to then and there take possession of the equipment described above from the respondent or his agents or employees or any other person who may be in possession thereof and deliver it to the petitioner.

Enclosed is our check in the amount of $45.00 as a deposit to cover your fees and any expenses. If you have any questions or problems, please contact the undersigned. Thank you for your assistance.

> Richard W. Todd, OSB #79421
> 430 Pacific Building
> 520 S.W. Yamhill St.
> Portland, OR 97204
> (503) 243-2035

Once the sheriff receives the writ of execution, the sheriff's instructions, the bond, and the appropriate fees, they will immediately go out to where the personal property is located and take it.

You do not need to accompany the sheriff on this trip. After they recover the property, it is transported to a bonded storage facility where it is kept until the time of sale. The sheriff then sets a date, time and place of sale — usually at the storage facility itself. They then send a notice of this sale to the defendant, to you and to any other interested parties.

"Interested parties" is an interesting term. It is not uncommon for the sheriff to take property in which someone has a security interest because money was borrowed to purchase it. There are also situations where the property seized is in fact only leased to the absent parent who has no ownership rights whatsoever. Property is sold without any guarantee of title other than a sheriff's certificate stating that he is authorized to sell it. Unless these lessors or secured parties come forward and contest the sale, they are usually out of luck as far as making a claim at a later date. Some great deals can be had at these sheriff's sales because they are not widely advertised, not well understood, and there is usually no opportunity to examine the property you are bidding on prior to the sale.

Since you have a judgment lien, you can bid on the personal property yourself up to the amount of your judgment without having to pay any cash. Anyone else has to pay cash if he or she is the successful bidder. Few people usually show up at these auctions as there is only one item at a time sold. Whatever monies are received are applied first to the cost of sale and then to your judgment. If the absent parent has a claim for exemption, there will be a hearing to determine how the proceeds are to be disbursed prior to the actual sale. Only the net proceeds recovered from the sale are applied to the judgment and not the fair market value of the property seized. Thus, if a car worth $3,000 is sold for only $50.00, only $50.00 is applied to the back child support and not the $3,000.

There are a couple of sub-species of the writ of execution that I will mention briefly. One is called a "till tap" and is quite effective when the absent parent owns a business that is open to the public and has a cash register. For approximately $35.00, the sheriff will go into the place of business and seize the contents of the cash register. For maximum effect, it is recommended that you do this during a busy time to maximize your recovery and emphasize to the absent parent the desirability to work with you in the future.

Another situation occurs where the personal property is actually in the hands of a third party. For example, the absent parent's car may be in the shop while the mechanic is doing some work. A writ of garnishment can be served on the mechanic to deliver the car to the sheriff similar to the garnishment of a bank account. In this case, the mechanic would be required to notify the sheriff that he has the car available for delivery to the sheriff and the same methods for recovery are utilized as in any other type of execution. This is seldom used and little understood by most people, including the sheriff himself. However, it can be quite a useful tool in those situations where it applies.

EXECUTION ON REAL PROPERTY

Unpaid child support can in all states constitute a judgment against the absent parent. The procedures in each state vary as to how to convert the unpaid child support into a judgment that can be recorded. Normally, the local child support enforcement office can provide you with specific information and an affidavit of default containing the amount of the child support arrearages. This is then filed with the clerk's office and becomes public record.

Any such judgment is a lien on any real property the absent parent owns in the county where the judgment is recorded.

If the absent parent owns real property, it is imperative to record in the county where the real property is located. If the property is located in a county different from the county where the judgment was obtained, you must request the court clerk to transfer the judgment to the county where the real property is located. Once recorded, the judgment automatically attaches to the real property and cannot be sold without you being paid the amount of the judgment.

Let's take an example. Assume the absent parent has purchased a home worth $80,000 and has a loan on it for $40,000. You have a child support judgment for $5,000. If he sells this property, the bank where he received the loan would receive their $40,000, you would receive your $5,000, and he would get the balance. This situation is becoming so common that title insurance companies are routinely listing divorce decrees and other child support orders as an exception to the title insurance policy. It is then up to the parent to obtain a release from the custodial parent in order for the sale to go through. This means that you must sign a document stating that he is current on the child support before the title insurance company will issue clear title to the property. If you refuse, the sale will normally not go through. Only by making arrangements with you will the sale be successful as no buyer is going to purchase property unless your judgment is satisfied. Otherwise, they purchase the property with your lien on it and you could foreclose eventually on them.

If the absent parent is not selling the property, the judgment remains on the property as a lien. You can foreclose on this lien and force the sale of the property if you feel there is sufficient equity to justify doing this. Foreclosure on real property is more complicated than the execution on personal property discussed above. I would not advise you to attempt this without the assistance of an attorney, although the procedure is similar to that of an execution on personal property.

The sheriff, after appropriate documents are submitted, takes control of the property and lists it for sale. The sale is usually advertised in the newspaper to reach prospective bidders. The buyer takes subject to any mortgages or other encumbrances and receives a deed from the sheriff. Any amounts bid are applied first to the cost of sale and then to your lien. There is usually a redemption right where the absent parent can pay the money within a certain period of time and keep the property. This can be a somewhat expensive procedure, but it's worth it if the absent parent has substantial equity in the property. My experience has been that you need only initiate this foreclosure and the absent parent will produce the money rather than lose his property.

Foreclosures on real property are statutory procedures which vary from state to state. If you do not wish to hire a private attorney, the local child support enforcement agency can be consulted to advise you as to whether it is appropriate in your particular case.

CREDITOR'S BILL

It is not uncommon for an absent parent to place his real or personal property into a corporate name or another individual's name to avoid your collection efforts. If an absent parent does this to avoid paying you, you can get such a transfer "set aside", or undone, because it is a fraudulent conveyance. Normally this is done through a procedure called a "creditor's bill". Basically, a creditor's bill is where you file a lawsuit against a third party to recover assets that rightfully belong to the absent parent. Lawsuits in this area are complicated and there is potential liability when suing a third party. It is advisable to seek the assistance of an attorney if you find yourself in this situation.

Through a creditor's bill, you sue the third person and request the court to attach the property that the absent parent has transferred to that third person. At a subsequent hearing or trial you will be called upon to provide evidence showing that the property belonged to the absent parent and that he transferred it into someone else's name to avoid your child support judgment. If you succeed, the judge will order the property turned over to the sheriff for sale pursuant to the execution procedure described earlier.

Hiring an attorney to file a creditor's bill is just like hiring an attorney to file any other kind of lawsuit. It can be very expensive and time consuming; results, of course, are not guaranteed. It is suggested that you utilize the contempt hearing procedures before hiring an attorney to file a creditor's bill. The contempt procedures will get the matter before the court more quickly and less expensively, often times with a better result. This is explored more fully in Chapter 8.

CHAPTER EIGHT

USING THE COURTS FOR HELP:

GARNISHMENT, EXECUTION AND WAGE WITHHOLDING

T
he biggest roadblock to obtaining information concerning the whereabouts of the absent parent and his assets is lack of cooperation. People may refuse to give you information for whatever reason; some people don't want you to know, some people won't take the time to help you, and some people are just plain suspicious about your motives. The most non-cooperative person is, of course, the absent parent, who resents your attempts to grab his assets and otherwise intrude upon his life.

Many delinquent fathers are not only uncooperative, they actively seek to conceal their assets and attempt to hide from you. Often times they enlist the aid of others to assist them. Bank accounts and titles to automobiles are placed in the name of their new spouse or close friends or relatives. Fictitious business names are used to conceal true ownership. It is not uncommon for persons who owe child support to quit their jobs and move on, rather than have a portion of their paycheck garnished to satisfy delinquent child support obligations.

When you are faced with problems such as the above, it is time to bring in the big guns of child support enforcement. Through the power of the subpoena, you can compel any individual or business to bring to you the documents you want to examine. Through a judgment debtor examination, you can compel the absent parent to appear in court and answer your questions regarding the amount and location of assets and other matters pertinent to your collection efforts. Through contempt of court proceedings, you can bring the absent parent before the judge who can order him to pay, to get a job, or to go to jail. Each of these procedures will be discussed in turn.

THE SUBPOENA

A subpoena is a written document signed by the clerk that orders a person to appear at a certain time and at a certain place so that you may ask them questions. Legally defined, a subpoena is a writ or order requiring the appearance of a person at a stated time and place for the taking of testimony. A subpoena "duces tecum" is a subpoena that requires not only the person to attend, but that person must bring along with him or her documents you specify or other tangible things. A subpoena allows you to compel uncooperative people to provide you with information and documents you need regarding your investigation and collection efforts.

Subpoenas are issued to secure attendance of witnesses at depositions or trials. A deposition is where you take the testimony of a witness before a court reporter in a question and answer format. Basically, you arrange for a room to take the deposition. This can be either at the courthouse (where rooms are often hard to reserve), at your office, or even at the office of the person to whom you are asking the questions. It can even be done at your home if you so desire. You also hire the court reporter, who records the questions and answers of your deposition for a fee (generally $25 to $50 per hour). For an additional fee, they can provide you with a transcript (written record) of the questions and answers for future reference. This can be fairly expensive and you should get a quote before ordering a transcript.

A subpoena has the force of a court order; failure to appear or otherwise respond can be grounds for contempt of court which can carry severe penalties. Most people are aware of the power of the subpoena; uncooperative people quickly become cooperative when served with one. After service of a subpoena on someone who has documents you need, these people will generally provide you with photocopies of the documents rather than taking the time to appear at a deposition. It is recommended that you contact the people you have subpoenaed after the subpoena has been served. Inquire if they will voluntarily provide the documents that you need or the information you seek to avoid the time and expense of a formal deposition. You will generally be able to work something out.

It is also a fact that people feel more comfortable providing information after they have been served with a subpoena. This is particularly true of persons who feel constrained by a particular relationship with the absent parent, for example, employer/employee or doctor/patient. When the irritated, delinquent father confronts these people after learning they have provided you information, they can merely shrug their shoulders and say "I had no choice. I was subpoenaed."

Any person who has information regarding your case, including the absent parent himself, may be subpoenaed. If the clerk of the court does not provide the subpoena forms, you can obtain them at your local business supply store. Every subpoena must have the name of the court from which it is issued, the title of the action, and the case number (collectively "the caption"). The language on the subpoena commands each person to whom it is directed to attend and give testimony or to produce and permit inspection and copying of designated books, documents or tangible things in the possession, custody or control of that person. Generally the subpoena form will contain all of the information that is required by the rules of civil procedure. You must only fill in the blanks of where you are going to hold the deposition, when you are going to have it, and what documents you want the witness to bring with him or her. The sample subpoena below is representative of all subpoenas used in the United States.

After you have filled in the blanks on the subpoena, you must take it to the clerk's office for them to sign it. There may be a small fee for this service (generally around $3.00). The subpoena is then considered "issued" and has the force and effect of an order from the court. You must then have someone serve the subpoena personally on the witness; it cannot be mailed or dropped off with his or her secretary in order to be effective.

SAMPLE 14: SUBPOENA

IN THE CIRCUIT COURT OF THE STATE OF OREGON
FOR THE COUNTY OF MULTNOMAH

JANE DOE,	)	
Plaintiff,	)	No. 0000-0000
	)	
v.	)	CIVIL SUBPOENA DUCES TECUM
	)	
JOHN DOE,	)	
Defendant.	)	

TO: Mike Witness
        520 Main St.
        Portland, Oregon

IN THE NAME OF THE STATE OF OREGON:
You are hereby required to appear on the 10th day of June, 1994, commencing at 1:00 p.m., in the offices of Saxon, Marquoit & Bertoni, 430 Pacific Building, 520 S.W. Yamhill Street, Portland, Oregon, for your deposition by the plaintiff, by and through counsel. You are required to appear and remain in attendance until the completion of your deposition. You are further required to bring with you any and all documents which are set forth on Exhibit A attached hereto and by reference incorporated herein.

ISSUED this _____ day of _____, 1994.

OFFICER OF THE COURT:

SAXON, MARQUOIT & BERTONI

RICHARD W. TODD, OSB #79421
Attorney for

You cannot serve the subpoena yourself. It can be served by any person other than yourself who is not less than 18 years of age. Procedurally, service is made upon a person by delivering a copy of the original subpoena to the person and also tendering to them the fees for attendance and the mileage allowed by law. The clerk can tell you the fee for attendance and the mileage allowance which is expressed as so much per mile. (Usually around $.10 per mile) Generally among states the appearance fee ranges from $5.00 to $25.00 per day.

After the subpoena is issued, make a copy of the subpoena; this copy will be your "service copy". Put the mileage fee and appearance fee in a blank envelope and staple it to the service copy. You then give the original and service copy to the person you are having serve it. After they have served the copy, they will fill out the back of the original subpoena indicating when and where it was served.

Generally speaking, a witness may be required to attend a deposition only in the county where he or she resides, is employed or transacts business. A person who resides outside of the state may only be required to attend in the county where the person is served with the subpoena or at a place fixed by court order. This limitation does not apply to the absent parent. Issuance of subpoenas to people who live in other states is a tricky process but it should be attempted anyway. Usually people will provide you with the information rather than fight the legitimacy of the subpoena.

JUDGMENT DEBTOR EXAMS

A judgment debtor exam is a proceeding where you can compel the absent parent to appear in court and answer your questions concerning the whereabouts of his employment, assets, and other matters that may assist you in collection. It is available when you have either tried to execute on an asset and were unsuccessful, or when you have sent a demand to pay the amount owed but he has failed to respond.

Although procedures may vary slightly from state to state, all have some type of judgment debtor exam relief. Some states have now instituted "written interrogatories" concerning the absent parent's property and financial affairs. Basically, written interrogatories are written questions that are delivered to the absent parent either personally or by certified mail. He must answer the questions truthfully and return the answers to you in writing within 20 days.

Judgment debtor exams and interrogatories can be more trouble than they are worth. If the absent parent fails to respond to the interrogatories or fails to appear at the judgment debtor exam hearing, you must commonly file yet another motion to "show cause" for contempt for failing to appear at the judgment debtor exam or failing to answer the written interrogatories. The order to show cause must then be served personally on the absent parent who must then appear at the date set in the show cause order. If he fails to appear at the show cause hearing, you can request that a bench warrant be issued for his arrest. If he is subsequently arrested, they will normally hold him in custody until you are able to appear in court to ask him the questions that you wish him to answer. Alternatively, he can post the bail set by the court (normally the amount of back child support owed) and you can levy on that bail.

These procedures sound good on paper, but in practice it can be very frustrating. Personal service on the absent parent is required and it is often difficult. It also requires numerous trips to the courthouse on your part and it can be expensive in terms of service fees. We include the procedure for conducting a judgment debtor exam together with examples of all the forms you will need in order to pursue it. We suggest, however, that you explore all alternatives before attempting it.

A court will generally not issue an order for an examination of an absent parent until; 1) there has been a return of service of an unsatisfied execution (see Chapter 7); or 2) the absent parent has been served with a notice of demand to pay the judgment and partial or full payment has not been received. This notice of demand can be in letter form; a sample is set forth on page 132.

The next step is to arrange for a time and place to have the judgment debtor exam hearing. The clerk of the court is the person to contact for this information. Because of the volume of judgment debtor exam hearings, they are normally all scheduled at one time before a certain judge on a certain day. All parties appear before the court at the time set. The judge calls off the names of the debtors, who then step forward and take an oath to testify to tell the truth. Normally, the debtor and the person asking the questions then goes out into the hall or into a jury room or other location where the questions are asked. If there is a dispute as to the type of question or the type of information sought, the parties can then go back into the courtroom and ask the judge for a ruling or clarification.

After a date and time is received from the court clerk, you must prepare a motion for examination of judgment debtor. The motion is normally supported by an affidavit setting forth that a notice of demand of judgment was sent or that an execution was returned unsatisfied. Examples of a motion with supporting affidavit are set forth on page 133 and 134.

You must also prepare an order for the judge to sign. The order must state that the absent parent is to appear before the court (in some states a referee appointed by the court) at the time and place specified in the order and answer under oath any questions regarding the absent parent's property. The order may also include a restraining order which restrains the absent parent from selling, transferring or disposing of any assets prior to the judgment debtor exam. Also, the order should state that the absent parent is to bring documents to examine. These can include federal and state income tax returns, check registers, check books, accounts receivable ledgers, and anything else you would like to examine that may be of assistance in your investigation. A sample order is set forth on page 135.

After the order is prepared, you need to take it to the court clerk who will give it to the judge to sign. After it is signed, request that the clerk provide you with a certified copy of the order for service upon the absent parent. It can then be delivered to the sheriff or a private process server for personal service upon the absent parent. Some states allow service by certified mail; when in doubt, however, opt for personal service.

If the absent parent resides out of town, send a letter to the sheriff in the county where the absent parent resides, together with the order and service fee, and tell him where and upon whom to serve the order and to notify you when the absent parent has been served.

SAMPLE 15: NOTICE OF DEMAND TO PAY JUDGMENT

IN THE CIRCUIT COURT OF THE STATE OF OREGON
FOR THE COUNTY OF MULTNOMAH

JANE DOE,	)	
	)	No. 000-000
Plaintiff,	)	
	)	
v.	)	NOTICE OF DEMAND TO
	)	PAY JUDGMENT
JOHN DOE,	)	
Defendant.	)	

TO: John Doe, 100 Main, Portland, Oregon, Defendant.

DEMAND IS HEREBY MADE upon you, pursuant to Oregon Revised Statutes, Section 23.710(1) for payment, within ten days of your receipt of this Notice, of that certain Judgment entered against you in the above court.

Payment may be made through the court or to the undersigned attorney at Plaintiff's offices.

PLEASE TAKE NOTICE THAT your failure to pay will result in further court proceedings.   TOTAL AMOUNT DUE: $15,000.00.
DATED this 1st day of April, 1994.

_____

Plaintiff or Plaintiff's Attorney

SAMPLE 16:   MOTION FOR EXAMINATION OF JUDGMENT DEBTOR

IN THE CIRCUIT COURT OF THE STATE OF OREGON
FOR THE COUNTY OF MULTNOMAH

JANE DOE,	)	
Plaintiff,	)	No. 000-000
	)	
v.	)	MOTION FOR EXAMINATION
	)	OF JUDGMENT DEBTOR
JOHN DOE,	)	
Defendant.	)	

Plaintiff moves for an order:

1.   Requiring <u>Defendant John Doe</u> to appear at a time and place to be fixed by the court and answer under oath questions concerning any property or interest in property that defendant may have or claim, (and then and there to produce the following documents of defendant:

_____
_____
_____
_____

2.   Restraining defendant from selling, transferring or in any manner disposing of his (its) property liable to execution, pending this proceeding.

This motion is based upon ORS 23.710, the records and files herein, and (choose one) (either) the return of service of an unsatisfied execution (or) proof of service on the attached affidavit of a notice of demand to pay the judgment within 10 days (or) proof of service on file herein of notice of demand to pay judgment within 10 days.

_____

Plaintiff or Attorney for Plaintiff

SAMPLE 17: AFFIDAVIT IN SUPPORT OF MOTION

IN THE CIRCUIT COURT OF THE STATE OF OREGON
FOR THE COUNTY OF MULTNOMAH

JANE DOE, 　　　Plaintiff,	)))	No.
v.	))	AFFIDAVIT IN SUPPORT OF MOTION
JOHN DOE, 　　　Defendant.	)))	
STATE OF OREGON County of Multnomah	)))	ss.

I, <u>Richard W. Todd</u>, being first duly sworn, depose and say that:

    1. I am one of plaintiff's attorneys.

    2. On or about April 1, 1994, I caused a notice of demand to pay judgment to be deposited in the U.S. Mail postage prepaid, in a sealed envelope addressed to <u>John Doe</u>, defendant, at <u>100 Main</u>, <u>Portland</u>, Oregon, by certified mail, return receipt requested.

    3. The notice of demand was served on defendant on <u>April 4, 1994</u>, as shown by the face of the receipt attached immediately below.

(attach copy of face of receipt here)

    4. A true copy of the notice of demand is attached hereto, marked "Exhibit A," and by this reference made part hereof.

_____
Attorney for Plaintiff

SUBSCRIBED AND SWORN to before me this _____ day of April, 1994.

_____
NOTARY PUBLIC FOR OREGON
My Commission Expires:_____

SAMPLE 18:   ORDER FOR EXAMINATION OF
              JUDGEMENT DEBTOR

IN THE CIRCUIT COURT OF THE STATE OF OREGON
FOR THE COUNTY OF MULTNOMAH

JANE DOE,	)	
Plaintiff,	)	No.
	)	
v.	)	ORDER FOR EXAMINATION
	)	OF JUDGMENT DEBTOR
JOHN DOE,	)	
Defendant.	)	

This matter coming on for hearing on plaintiff's motion for examination of judgment debtor, and it appearing from the records and files herein that the judgment in this matter is unsatisfied and (choose one) (either) an execution herein has been returned unsatisfied (or) a notice of demand to pay judgment within 10 days has been served upon defendant in a manner provided by law, it is hereby

ORDERED that <u>John Doe</u> appear before the presiding judge of the above-entitled court in Room No. _____ of the Multnomah County Courthouse, Portland, Oregon, on the _____ day of _____, 1994, at the hour of _____,_.m., and answer under oath questions concerning any property or interest in property that defendant may have or claim, and it is further

ORDERED that <u>Defendant</u> then and there produce the following documents of defendant: _____,

_____

_____

_____

and it is further

ORDERED that defendant be, and hereby is, restrained from selling, transferring, or in any manner disposing of any of his (her) (its) property liable to execution pending this proceeding.

DATED this _____ day of April, 1994.

_____

CIRCUIT COURT JUDGE

As stated above, the oral examination is usually held at the courthouse because the judge is handy to order the debtor to turn over or apply certain disclosed assets in satisfaction of the judgment. A court reporter is optional to take down the answers to your questions. The decision to use a reporter should weigh the expense versus the possible impression it may make upon the absent parent. Write all the questions out that you want to ask in advance, or use the list below.

SAMPLE QUESTIONS: ORAL DEBTOR'S EXAMINATION

DATE: NAME OF COURT REPORTER:

1. PERSONAL

    A. Full Name:
    B. Residence address:
    C. Residence telephone number:
    D. Spouse's name, occupation, and employer:
    E. How many children under age 18?

2. OCCUPATION

    A. Employer or name of business:
    B. Type of business:
    C. Your occupation:
    D. Business address:
    E. Business telephone number:
    F. Business associates (if any):
    G. Name of employer's bank, address:
    H. Employment history for past 3 years:

3. INCOME

    A. Income from occupation or business:
    B. Income from all other sources, including pensions, disability, unemployment, and other businesses:
    C. Commissions or renewals earned or anticipated:
    D. Pertinent information from Oregon and federal tax returns and other books and records brought to examination:

4. INTERESTS IN REAL PROPERTY

    A. Beneficial or fee interest:

    B. Amount of equity in your home, and who holds mortgage:

    C. Purchaser or seller on contract: With whom? How much is owed?:

    D. Lessor or lessee:

    E. Remainder or contingent interest:

    F. Beneficial use of any real property in the name of another, including spouse:

    G. Mortgage, or beneficiary under deed of trust:

    H. Any other interest whatever in real property in Oregon or any other state or country:

5. SECURITIES

    A. Stock:

        1. If a shareholder in a close corporation, is the debtor an officer or director?

        2. Who are the other officers, directors and major shareholders?

        3. Any other stock:

        4. Any accounts with brokerage houses:

    B. Debt:

        1. Checks, drafts, or notes payable to the debtor:

        2. Bonds, dividends, certificates, certificates of deposit, deposits, or other interest-bearing instruments:

6. CASH EQUIVALENT

    A. Cash on hand:

    B. Safe deposit boxes:

    C. Bank, savings and loan, and credit union accounts of any kind:

    D. Deposits of money with any other institution or person:

    E. Cash value on insurance policies:

    F. IRS and state tax refunds due or expected:

7. CHOSES IN ACTION

    A. Accounts receivable or debts on open account

    B. Liquidated or unliquidated claims of any nature, including in contract and tort:

    C. Claims against insurance companies:

    D. Security interests and other liens or claims:

8. **OTHER PERSONAL PROPERTY**

   A. Household goods:
   B. Automobiles, trucks, motorcycles, and other vehicles:
   C. Boat or other vessel: How much is owed on it?
   D. Inventory, tools, machinery, and fixtures:
   E. Farm equipment, animals or crops:
   F. Jewelry or other valuable property including sculpture, paintings, antiques, stamps, coins, etc.:
   G. Patents, copyrights, trademarks, trade names, royalties, etc.:
   H. Any documents of title, including warehouse receipts, etc.:
   I. Any interest in any other business, partnership, or joint venture:
   J. Real estate listings:
   K. Any licenses or permits from public authorities:
   L. Any other property, tangible or intangible, which might have potential value:

9. **TRUSTS, ETC.**

   A. Is any property held for you in trust, guardianship, conservatorship, or custodianship?
   B. Are you a trustee, custodian, guardian or conservator?
   C. Are you an heir of anyone who has passed away?

10. **LEGAL PROCEEDINGS**

   A. Do you now have a legal claim against any party or does any party now have a legal claim against you?
   B. Have you been a party to any legal proceeding over the past three years?
      1. If so, have you satisfied any judgment against you?
      2. Has there been a levy against any of your property?
      3. Has any third party satisfied a judgment for you?
      4. Have you collected any judgment?
   C. In the past three years, has the IRS or any state or county agency asserted a claim for unpaid taxes against you?

11. **OTHER INDEBTEDNESS**

   A. Names and addresses of secured creditors and amounts claimed by each:
   B. Names and addresses of unsecured creditors and amounts claimed by each, including tax collectors:
   C. Names and addresses of judgment creditors, amount of each judgment:

D. Names and addresses of those to whom you have applied for a loan in the past 3 years:

12. TRANSFERS AND LOSSES

A. Transfers of property within the past 2 years to relatives, charities, trusts, or others:

B. Money deposited in accounts in the name of another over the past 2 years:

C. Loans repaid over the past 2 years:

D. Assignments of payments, notes, contracts, insurance policies, or wages over the past 2 years:E.Purchases of property, including stock, for another over the past 2 years:

F. Conveyances of real property over the past 2 years:

G. Losses of any sort over the past 2 years:

H. Transfers of any property over past 2 years, not in the usual course of business:

I. Does anyone else hold title to or possession of any property in which you have any rights or interest?

13.   BOOKS AND RECORDS

A. Name and address of accountant-bookkeeper:

If examination reveals non-exempt assets (as discussed in Chapter 7), immediately go into the court and ask the judge for an order requiring the absent parent to turn that asset over to the sheriff to be held for execution and sale. If the debtor fails to appear at the examination, you must proceed through the contempt procedures discussed earlier. Some courts will immediately issue a bench warrant for his arrest, but the more common procedure is to request a show cause hearing for contempt. If you find yourself in this situation, you are probably better off to proceed with the contempt procedure as described in the next section.

CONTEMPT PROCEEDINGS

Contempt proceedings are the strongest enforcement technique that you have available to you. It is the traditional method of child support enforcement and the most effective. Often times it is the only tool you have available to enforce support orders against those who are self-employed, work "under the table," or who choose to be intermittently employed, if at all. It basically says to the absent parent: "Either pay up or go to jail."

An order to pay child support is just that: a court order. Willful failure to comply with that court order is a contempt of court; the ultimate sanction for contempt is time in jail. There is "civil contempt" and there is "criminal contempt". For the purposes of our discussion, they will be treated as one and the same.

Initiating a contempt proceeding is similar to that of a judgment debtor exam or modification proceeding. You must file a motion for an order to show cause why the absent parent should not be held in contempt of court, together with your affidavit setting forth the reasons for the contempt. You can do this yourself, you can have a private attorney do it, or you can have a government attorney do it. Regardless of who does it, the procedure is the same and the forms are normally preprinted because of the volume of these types of proceedings. Ask the clerk of the court if such a form is used and where you may obtain it. A sample motion affidavit and order is set out on page 144 through 146.

As you can see from the sample affidavit on page 145, the facts constituting the contempt must be set forth. These facts are fairly simple:

1. That an order was entered by the court requiring the absent parent to pay child support;

2. The amount of child support that was ordered;

3. The amount of child support that has been paid;

4. The amount of child support owed as of the date of this affidavit;

It is normally a good idea (and in some jurisdictions required) that a schedule of the child support payments be attached to your affidavit.

After these forms are prepared, present them to the clerk at the courthouse to obtain a date for the contempt hearing. Once again, ask for a certified copy of the order to show cause and make arrangements for the absent parent to be served with this certified copy. Either the sheriff or a process server will do, but the order must be served in person.

At the time of the hearing, you must prove by your testimony the facts contained in your affidavit. The court will take notice of your order to pay child support because it will be on file and you need only refer to it (see Chapter 1 if this is not the court where you received your divorce or paternity order). The remaining elements can be proved by your testimony: the payments he has not made and the amount that he currently owes.

The only defense to a finding of contempt of court is the absent parent's financial inability to pay child support. For example, he may have become ill or disabled and that has rendered him unable to maintain employment in which to pay the support. On the other hand, it is not a defense that the absent parent has so many personal expenses that there is not money left over to pay his child support. The most common defense is that the absent parent is unemployed and has been unable to find work, although the stories and excuses are often times quite creative.

Willful failure to pay child support can result in jail time and the absent parent is entitled to court-appointed counsel if he is unable to retain his own attorney. Frequently the attorney will advise him to not testify on fifth amendment grounds, i.e. that he may incriminate himself. Such a position will undoubtedly lead to a finding of contempt anyway.

Proving contempt is very simple. The result of a contempt is where the weakness of the contempt proceeding is exposed. Some courts still feel that the failure to pay child support is relatively unimportant; as a result, no real penalty is imposed. It is not uncommon for a person to bring numerous actions for contempt before any significant action is taken by the court. If you have had to bring a contempt action in the past, it is important that you bring this up with the court as the penalties generally increase with each successive contempt action. Courts routinely let the absent parent off with a lecture or warning which the absent parent routinely ignores.

This, of course, requires repeated trips to the courthouse, a repeated time commitment on your part, and repeated costs in issuance and service fees. It is extremely aggravating, to say the least.

Coupled with the failure of the court to strictly enforce the terms of the support orders are the efforts of the absent parents' attorneys to continually seek continuances of the contempt hearings. With rare exception, it is unwise to agree to any continuance unless they pay you money to do it. It is this author's experience that a continuance to allow the absent parent to come up with the money almost never works, and more likely than not will worsen your position. Increasingly, the court will order the absent parent to find employment if he does not have a job. They will then reset the hearing for a future date at which time the absent parent either must pay child support, get a job and pay child support, or provide proof at the subsequent hearing of his efforts to locate employment.

It is not uncommon for courts to order payment of the current child support and a percentage of the back child support. For example, assume a monthly child support obligation of $200.00 with back child support owed in the amount of $2,500. The court will order the absent parent to pay $225.00 per month. $200 is for the current monthly child support obligation and $25.00 is applied to the $2,500 arrearage. So long as the absent parent meets that schedule, he will not be held in contempt for failure to pay the entire arrearage. This is hardly an acceptable arrangement for the custodial parent. She is forced to accept $25.00 per month on an obligation of $2,500 which will take years to pay off. Realistically, however, it may be the best you're going to get.

Statistically, most absent parents have the ability to pay, but just choose not to. All things considered, the contempt hearing is worth the time and effort because it shows the absent parent that you are not going to let him "slide" on his obligation. Even though it consumes your time, it also consumes his in a way he might not like it spent. It is very humiliating to be "dressed down" by a judge in front of an ex-spouse, and few men care to repeat it. Also, even if you have to take him to court a dozen times for contempt, there is a certain satisfaction in seeing him pay the ultimate price by being sent to jail.

Most of the contempt hearings in this country are done on behalf of the custodial parent by the district attorney's office. They generally go in once a week and do a number of them at the same time. If you become part of that group, you have to wait your turn for a contempt hearing to be scheduled. These government attorneys generally know their business but they are extremely busy because of the volume of their caseload. They will often grant continuances and make other deals without your permission. If you use one, be prepared for some frustration.

The costs of a private attorney can often times exceed the amount of child support you collect. However, a court will frequently order the absent parent to pay your attorney fees for having to bring the contempt action in the first place. If you can collect these attorney fees from the absent parent, it's worth it. However, it will be just as difficult to collect the attorney fees as it will be to collect the back child support.

Whether you pursue contempt hearings with the assistance of an attorney or not, it is important that you utilize this collection tool. Statistical evidence from all over the country consistently shows that the threat of jail raises both the amount of child support collected and the frequency of payment. The psychological effect is extremely powerful and generally produces better results than any other procedure available to you.

SAMPLE 19: MOTION AND AFFIDAVIT FOR ORDER TO SHOW CAUSE RE: CONTEMPT

IN THE CIRCUIT COURT OF THE STATE OF OREGON
FOR THE COUNTY OF MULTNOMAH

In the Matter of the Marriage of:	)
	) No. 90DO-1082DS
JANE DOE	)
Petitioner,	)
	) MOTION AND AFFIDAVIT
and	) FOR ORDER TO SHOW CAUSE
	) RE: CONTEMPT
JOHN DOE,	)
Respondent.	)

MOTION

Petitioner moves for an order requiring respondent to appear and show cause, if any there be, why petitioner should not be held in contempt of court for failing to comply with the provisions of the Judgment and Decree of Dissolution of Marriage previously entered herein on or about September 14, 1990, as specifically alleged in the affidavit set forth hereinbelow.

Pursuant to TOCR 2, petitioner declares that:

1. The maximum sanction petitioner seeks is an order incarcerating respondent in the county jail until he complies with the order of the court by paying child support to petitioner.

2. Petitioner seeks a sanction of confinement.

3. Petitioner considers this sanction to be remedial.

Petitioner also moves the court for judgment against respondent on account of petitioner's reasonable attorney fees and actual costs incurred herein supported by petitioner's affidavit as set forth hereinbelow.

DATED this _____ day of April, 199.

SAXON, MARQUOIT & BERTONI
Richard W. Todd, OSB #79421
Of Attorneys for Petitioner

AFFIDAVIT

STATE OF OREGON	)	
	)	ss.
County of Multnomah	)	

I, _____, hereby swear the following to be true: I am the petitioner herein. Respondent is my former husband. We were divorced pursuant to a Judgment and Decree of Dissolution of Marriage entered herein on or about September 14, 1990.

Paragraph 6 of the court's judgment reads as follows:

"6. That respondent is hereby ordered to pay support to petitioner in the amount of $300 per month for the care, support and maintenance of said minor child, payable through the Oregon Department of Human Resources in monthly installments of $300 each on the 15th of each month, until each child is emancipated in accordance with Oregon State Law, and is no longer attending school on a regular basis. All support payments shall be in the form of cash or check made payable to Support Services, with the first such installment to be paid on or before September 15, 1990.

Respondent has failed and refused to pay any child support as ordered by the court despite repeated demand that he do so.

Based on the above, I believe respondent is in willful contempt of the decree of dissolution and therefore I ask that he be adjudged in contempt of court. In addition, I ask that the court impose all of the following sanctions, all of which I consider to be remedial in nature:

a. Requiring respondent to pay a sum of money sufficient to compensate me for loss, injuries, or costs suffered by me as a result of respondent's contempt of court;

b. Confining respondent in the Multnomh County Jail or other appropriate facility for so long as his contempt continues, or six months whichever is shorter;

c. Requiring respondent to pay an amount not to exceed $500, or 1% of his annual gross income, whichever is greater, for each day he remains in contempt of court. I ask the court that this sanction be imposed to compensate me for the effects of his continuing contempt.

d. Any order designed to insure compliance with a prior order of the court including probation.

e. Any other additional sanction if the court determines that the sanction would be an effective remedy for the contempt.

145

f. Awarding me a judgment against respondent for all of my attorney fees, costs, and disbursements incurred in this matter pursuant to ORS 33.105(1)(e).

_____, Petitioner

SUBSCRIBED AND SWORN to before me this _____ day of April, 1994.

_____
NOTARY PUBLIC FOR OREGON
My Commission Expires:_____

SAMPLE 20: ORDER TO SHOW CAUSE RE: CONTEMPT

IN THE CIRCUIT COURT OF THE STATE OF OREGON
FOR MULTNOMAH COUNTY
Department of Domestic Relations

STATE OF OREGON, ex rel,	)
	) No.
JANE DOE,	) DA. No. 5001
Plaintiff,	)
	) ORDER TO APPEAR TO ANSWER
v.	) CONTEMPT OF COURT
	) CHARGE - FAILURE TO OBEY
JOHN DOE,	) SUPPORT ORDER
Defendant.	)

TO:

On the Motion of the Plaintiff,

YOU ARE ORDERED TO APPEAR in person before the Court, Multnomah County Courthouse, 1021 S.W. Fourth Avenue, Portland, Oregon, and show cause why you should not be adjudged guilty of contempt of Court for disobeying the support order entered in the above-entitled Court and cause.

_____ BE PREPARED TO TESTIFY REGARDING
_____ YOUR FINANCIAL POSITION. BRING
_____ WITH YOU ANY RECORDS YOU MAY
_____ HAVE IN CONNECTION WITH YOUR
_____ INCOME, ASSETS, EXPENSES AND
_____ SUPPORT PAYMENTS

NOTICE TO DEFENDANT: You are entitled to be represented by an attorney at the Court hearing. If you desire an attorney but cannot afford one, the Court will appoint legal counsel for you.

Dated this _____ day of May, 1994

_____
Circuit Court Judge

CHAPTER NINE

USING THE GOVERNMENT FOR HELP

TITLE IV AND THE IRS

I f you are receiving welfare, you have already assigned your rights to child support over to the state. The state is essentially paying you child support on behalf of the absent parent and, with certain exceptions, will reimburse itself from that absent parent for the payments they make to you. If you are not receiving welfare and are not receiving child support payments from the absent parent, you should consider using the services of your local Child Support Enforcement Agency to help you collect money from him. Appendix A is a list of addresses and telephone numbers of all the local support enforcement offices in the United States.

You have the right to use the local child support enforcement agency whether you can afford an attorney or not. These government agencies locate absent parents, establish paternity, establish and enforce support orders, and collect child support payments. While the programs vary from state to state, their services are available to all custodial parents who request them. It is usually administered through state and county local services departments, although many states contract with local prosecuting attorneys and other law enforcement agencies to carry out the program at the local level. It is funded primarily by the federal government who basically created the program to get back from absent parents the money they were spending on welfare. It has since been expanded to include non-welfare mothers. Although the services for the most part are free, the states can charge a maximum fee of $25.00.

As we will see in this chapter, the government offers a wide variety of services and, in the area of child support, offers "one-stop shopping". If you do not have a child support order, they will obtain one for you. If you do not know the location of the absent parent, they will seek that information for you as well. If he is not paying, they will act as your attorney to seek enforcement through all of the measures we have discussed in this book.

That is what the governmental agencies are supposed to do. As a practical matter, it rarely works efficiently except in those cases where collection is relatively easy. After all, federal guidelines are only as good as the individual caseworker who is handling your particular file. Among the problems that people have experienced are as follows:

1. A mother fills out an application for services but never hears from the agency again.

2. Some agencies will not allow phone calls to your caseworker, letters to the agencies go unanswered and one merely sits and waits in the hope that information is provided. In one reported case, a woman was told that if she made any more phone calls, her file would be "lost".

3. Caseworkers in different counties may not speak to one another to decide which county should handle the case when a parent has moved within the state. Each county points the finger at the other; the result is no services to the parent.

4. In interstate cases, attorneys and caseworkers in the second state will speak only with the caseworker from the first state. Caseworkers in the first state either refuse to speak to the second state or lack the budget to make long-distance telephone calls. Some caseworkers lack infor-

mation regarding new laws and get very snippy when you try to point them out.

5. Many caseworkers fail to explain possible sources of collecting money, such as tax refund intercepts. Some mothers who have inquired have even been told that such options are not available to them because they were not on welfare (not true).

Most child support enforcement offices have an abundance of cases and many have more than they can handle efficiently. As a rule, your case gets no particular priority and you can expect the whole procedure to take months to get rolling. It is unrealistic to expect your case to be handled in the same fashion or with the same efficiency that you would receive with a private attorney; in fact, you should never assume that someone is actively working on your case within the government. Included in this chapter is, therefore, a section on ensuring that your case is not forgotten.

In spite of these problems, governmental agencies do produce results and they have the decided advantage of access to records that you cannot touch. This chapter will highlight those areas where the government can be of most assistance in spite of the problems and delays you may encounter.

EXPEDITED ADMINISTRATIVE PROCESSES TO ESTABLISH AND ENFORCE CHILD SUPPORT OBLIGATIONS

In Chapter 5, we discussed parent locator services offered by the government. In addition to these state parent locater services, each state is required to have "expedited processes" in place to obtain and enforce support orders and to establish paternity. These procedures to establish child support are normally done through an administrative process, but they still have the same force and effect as orders obtained through the court. In addition, this administrative process must be available for interstate cases and in those situations where no public assistance is being granted.

What all this means is that the government can obtain a child support order for you without going to court. The process is commenced by the issuance of a "notice of financial responsibility" to the absent parent. Typically, it contains the following information:

- Names and birthdates of the children;
- whether or not public assistance (welfare) is being paid and the total amount owed by the absent parent to the state for that public assistance;
- an explanation of the absent parent's rights regarding the administrative order and the fact that a default order will be entered if the absent parent does not respond to the notice.

Once the notice is received, the absent parent has a certain amount of time to respond. If he does nothing, the support order is automatically established by default and may then be enforced. Alternatively, the absent parent may want to discuss the support obligation with the support enforcement caseworker and they may agree upon a certain amount of support. This results in a "stipulated" administrative support order. Failure to comply with that order will also result in enforcement.

The third alternative is that the absent parent may request a hearing regarding the support amount. This will normally be heard by an administrative hearings officer who will enter an order which may be appealed to the courts. If appealed to the courts, it is handled as described in Chapter 1.

Federal law requires that this administrative order, however obtained, must have the same force and effect as orders established by a court. In those states where it is available, this is the preferred way to get a support order established because you avoid the inevitable delays which result from having to file documents with a court clerk, waiting for a judge to review the various orders, and waiting to schedule hearings at a future date on cases where the absent parent does not appear anyway. Costs are also reduced, since it is normally not necessary to use attorneys or the courts.

The amount of child support awarded in administrative hearings is identical to what you would obtain in court hearings. Virtually all states now use a matrix system of some type (Chapter 2) and you will not receive lower child support because you take the "administrative route" to obtain it. Once the order is obtained, the state will, upon request, move forward with the various enforcement procedures discussed in this book. Payments are made to them and forwarded on to you, resulting in accurate recordkeeping. Such a procedure has the added benefit of reducing the time you must spend in court on the collection efforts. If the payments have been made through the Support Enforcement Agency, their records of payments can be used in court hearings and you do not normally have to appear in court to testify regarding any child support delinquency.

WAGE WITHHOLDING ORDERS

Once a support order is monitored by the local Child Support Enforcement Agency, they will immediately institute a wage withholding order if the child support becomes more than one month overdue. This is mandatory under federal law, even in situations where the absent parent makes partial payments. In many states, this procedure has now become computerized and the computer will automatically send out a wage withholding order when its records show that the absent parent is one month behind.

Commencing in 1994, all new or modified support orders will require that child support payments be withheld from the absent parent's wages automatically, regardless of whether the absent parent is in arrears. All child support obligations will be determined according to the support guidelines and will be reviewed by the Child Support Enforcement Agency every three years. This automatic review will only be available to you if the absent parent is making payments through the state. If he is paying you directly, there would, of course, be no such review. This is an additional reason for you to have the payments made through the state rather than directly to you.

If you would like the Child Support Enforcement Agency to obtain a wage deduction order, you must complete an application for child support services if you have not already done so. Be prepared to provide the following information:

a. Full name, address and telephone number of absent parent, if known;
b. social security number;
c. name and address of employer, if known;
d. the court order or judgment which shows your right to receive child support;
e. any information you have regarding the absent parent's income.

Normally, you will then be assigned a caseworker who will attempt contact with the absent parent. If that is not available or undesirable, a demand letter will be sent stating that, if the child support payments are not made, a wage withholding order will be sent to the employer. Some states are dispensing with this prerequisite and are immediately filing a wage deduction order. If this is the case in your state, or in other states if the absent parent ignores the letter, he will receive formal notice of a wage deduction order. This notice is given before the agency sends the order to the employer. He then has a certain amount of time—normally ten days—to object to the order. If a mistake has been made, or if he is in fact current, he will have time to prevent the imposition of the order with his employer. Absent such a legitimate objection, the notice is delivered to the employer and goes into effect immediately. The employer must comply with the order or risk paying the child support amount out of the employer's own pocket.

A wage withholding order does not take the absent parent's entire paycheck. In most states, the order requires that the employer deduct twenty-five percent (25%) of his net take-home pay and send it to the Support Enforcement Agency. The wage withholding remains in effect until the children reach the age of majority, the absent parent changes jobs, or it is withdrawn by the agency. If the wage withholding order also seeks collection of back child support, it will remain in effect until the total arrearage has been paid, regardless of whether the children reach the age of majority.

If the absent parent has a steady job, the wage withholding order is probably the most effective procedure to collect unpaid child support. Most employers are accustomed to these orders if they have an appreciable number of employees and are usually timely in submitting them to the state. If the absent parent transfers to another job, the employer is required to provide this information to the state so that a new withholding order can be put into place. If there are substantial arrearages, the amount to be withheld cannot be less than twenty-five percent (25%) of the obligor's disposable income and cannot exceed the maximum amount permitted under the Consumer Protection Act (50%-65% of disposable earnings, depending on the facts in each case). Once the arrearages are paid in full, the amount to be withheld normally equals the monthly support obligation plus an employer fee (approximately $1.00 to $5.00 per check).

TAX REFUND INTERCEPT

The federal tax refund intercept program has been very successful since it was implemented in 1981. It is estimated that the government has intercepted almost $1 billion dollars in back child support which accounts for approximately twenty percent (20%) of all support recovered during the last four years. In 1985, for example, over 490,000 refunds were offset for payment of child support totalling $240,000,000. The average amount collected was approximately $500, with an average cost of $3.20 per case.

Although the tax refund intercept can only be instituted through the government child support agency, anyone who is owed at least $150 in back child support can utilize it. However, the agency will not automatically utilize this tool and you must request that they do so.

To intercept the absent parent's federal tax refund, you must be registered with your local child support agency and have a support obligation in affect. They normally will require you to sign an affidavit attesting to the amount of support owed and they must know the absent parent's address. The reason for this is, once again, the absent parent receives written advance notice of the government's intent to divert the tax refund check to them and provide an opportunity for him to contest the intercept. If a mistake has been made, then it can be corrected before the intercept goes into effect.

Every August, each state submits to the IRS a list of all cases together with the amount of their arrearages. The advance notice of the intercept is sent by the IRS and the only basis for contesting it is that the wrong taxpayer has been named or the amount of child support is incorrect. It is not a defense to the intercept that the taxpayer is complying with an order to pay a specific amount towards the arrearage. After the refund is intercepted, the taxpayer will be notified and the intercepted money will be sent to the child support agency for disbursement to you.

If the absent parent filed a joint return with someone else, the entire joint refund will be taken even if an objection is raised by the new spouse. The IRS has a procedure for the non-debtor's spouse to obtain their share of the refund after it has been intercepted. The amount of their refund is based on a formula utilizing their relative share of the income on that return. An additional problem occurs on those returns where there is an earned income credit. The refund based on an earned income credit is seized as well, but this situation may change in the future.

Because of the success of the federal program, many states are using a similar intercept program on state income tax refunds due delinquent absent parents. If the absent parent lives in a state where a state income tax return is required, inquiry should be made to determine whether a state tax intercept is available.

IRS FULL COLLECTION PROCEDURES

When everything else fails, the IRS full collection service and use of 1099 asset information should be requested. This procedure is particularly effective to collect from self-employed individuals where wage withholding is unavailable or impractical. In essence, this procedure unleashes the Internal Revenue Service on the absent parent; even the threat of this produces results.

To implement the IRS full collection procedure, you must be eligible for welfare or have applied for services with the local Support Enforcement Agency. The Support Enforcement Agency must have made efforts to collect the debt and must agree to reimburse the IRS for the costs of collection. There must be an existing administrative order or court order for support and the amount to be collected must be at least $750. At least six months must have elapsed since the last request for IRS assistance and sufficient information must be supplied to identify the debtor. Finally, there must be reason to believe that the debtor has assets that the Secretary of the Treasury might levy upon to collect the support.

Once these requirements have been met, the IRS may proceed to enforce the support obligations in the same manner and with the same power as if the child support amount were a tax. Basically, this means that the delinquency is sent to a district IRS office and the account is referred to a revenue officer for collection. The IRS officer will attempt to contact the absent parent to obtain a financial statement and to arrange a payment agreement. Failing this, a notice of intent to levy may issue and the IRS can enforce collection against any income or assets of debtor except certain exempt property. The fee for this collection service is $122.50.

Despite the awesome power of this collection device, only a few thousand referrals have been made to the IRS in the last ten years. Of these few thousand, only about 100 cases resulted in any collections, but the average return was $10,000. A few individual cases resulted in recoveries of $20,000-$30,000. If you have a lot of money owing, this procedure should be insisted upon.

The Internal Revenue Service is also utilized to obtain disclosure of certain return information to aid in locating absent parents. The IRS has agreed to conduct quarterly matches of absent parent names and social security numbers submitted on magnetic tape with the 1099 wage and information document master file. This 1099 information includes the address which the absent parent has reported to the reporting institution, and the address of the submitting institution (such as banks, stock brokerages, money market funds, etc.) In addition to the addresses, the states will receive accompanying asset information whenever there is a match on the computer.

Requests for 1099 location information can only be made where the Support Enforcement Agency has previously requested location information from the IRS, but is still unable to locate the absent parent. Although the 1099 will reveal information concerning the absent parent's assets such as bank accounts, this information is provided only for the purpose of locating the absent parent and cannot be passed on to enforcement officers to assist in execution against the assets that are discovered. Therefore, the states that use this system must certify that they have a security system to prevent the information from being misused. (I agree, the logic here is questionable.)

States can circumvent this nondisclosure requirement by independently verifying the 1099 information through subpoenaing the banks and other conventional methods. Unfortunately, only a handful of states have bothered to comply with the IRS requirements for 1099 information; hopefully this usage will improve in the future.

The IRS is also compiling 1098 information (the record of interest paid by taxpayers) which could be useful in the future to locate absent parents. It will have the same limitations, however, in that access to this information will only be for the purpose of location and not for asset identification.

THE FIFTY DOLLAR DISREGARD AND AFDC

Normally, the outside income of the family reduces the family's welfare assistance on a dollar-for-dollar basis. Congress has carved out an exception to this general rule by disregarding the first fifty dollars of child support received by the family. In other words, when a family is applying for or receiving AFDC, the first fifty dollars of any child support payment received in the month will be paid to the family and disregarded as income for AFDC purposes.

In addition to the fifty dollar disregard, many custodial parents and their children will need to receive public benefits after their divorce to provide minimally adequate living conditions. The benefits available to you are primarily medicaid, food stamps and AFDC. Medicaid provides health care coverage for you and your children if you are unemployed or if you are employed at a job that does not provide health benefits. Food stamps are coupons which can be used to purchase groceries for you and your children; AFDC is a cash payment to help you and your family meet your basic living expenses.

If you are eligible for AFDC, you are automatically eligible for Medicaid. To be eligible for AFDC, you must have in your family a child who is deprived of parental care because one of his or her parents is dead, disabled of absent from the home, have few resources and limited income. Normally speaking, you cannot have more than $1,000 in non-exempt resources to be eligible for AFDC. You can have a home, household goods and a car worth less than $1,500.

All other assets will be counted toward the $1,000 amount. If you are receiving income, most of the time that amount will be deducted from the AFDC grant except, of course, for the first $50 of support paid each month.

After the first $50, the balance of cash support paid by the absent parent goes to the state to reimburse it for the AFDC grant. A loophole has been carved out for what is called in-kind payments which may not be considered as income deductible from the AFDC grant. For example, if the absent parent buys the child's clothes, pays for child care, or makes some other type of direct payment, such payments may be exempt for the purposes of reducing your AFDC. If you find yourself in that type of situation, you should discuss it with an attorney who specializes in this area for more specific information.

If you have less that $1,500 in non-exempt assets, you should also be eligible for food stamps, even if you are not otherwise eligible for AFDC. The following assets are not counted when determining eligibility for food stamps: the family home, household goods, cash value of life insurance and pension plan, and some vehicles. Eligibility for food stamps also depends on you having a low income; currently, all child support paid is counted as income to you. Once again, if the support is in the nature of rent payments or something similar, these payments may not be considered as income. Consult a local expert if you find yourself in this situation.

CONCLUSION

Keep in touch with your child support enforcement office. Do not harass them with telephone calls, but call them frequently so that your case does not get put on the back burner. Depending on the relationship you have with your caseworker, you should call once every two weeks for a status report and more frequently if information is not forthcoming.

If you are not satisfied with the the assistance you are receiving from the local agency, you should write a letter of complaint to the head of the local child support office with copies to the state and regional offices. The letters should be brief and to the point; state that the agency has failed to properly take action on your case and request information as to what is being done.

If no one has written back to you within two weeks, you should contact your local U.S. Senator or U.S. Representative's office and request an inquiry. In addition, there are several self-help groups listed in Appendix B that can help you put pressure on getting some action on your case. Persistence is the key to collection, even with respect to people who are on your side.

Special Situations

CHAPTER TEN

Collecting Money in
Other States and Countries

I t is no secret that the easiest way to avoid financial obligations is to get as far away as possible from the person trying
to collect it. The most difficult child support cases to pursue
are where the absent parent lives in another state or country.
Obtaining the support order is easy compared to enforcing the
support order when the person owing money is not in the immedi-
ate vicinity.

Fortunately, our government has recognized the ease in
which a husband or boyfriend could abandon his children and has
passed legislation to assist in collection. Keep in mind, however,
that the support order you have (or need to get if you don't
already have one) is an order from a state and not from the federal
government. Each state has its own unique court system with its
own laws, traditions, and practices. Domestic relations matters,
including the payment of child support, have always been considered the responsibility of state and local governments in the areas
where the children live. You can, therefore, only use the tools and

enforcement techniques that the state where the absent parent lives allows you to use.

There are four primary legal tools for interstate enforcement of child support:

1. The Uniform Reciprocal Enforcement of Support Act (URESA)
2. Interstate Income Withholding
3. The Uniform Enforcement of Foreign Judgments Act
4. "Long Arm" Statutes

There is really no federal law for support enforcement, and the federal government has shown a surprising lack of concern for the problems of child support and child custody, both national and international. The theory is that this problem is "local" in nature, and even though the obligation of parents to support their children is a universal belief, no treaties currently exist between the United States and other countries that specifically address this problem. There are several international treaties that address the enforcement of support obligations when the debtor and creditor are in countries other than the United States, including the United Nations Convention on the Recovery Abroad of Maintenance, the 1958 Hague Convention Concerning the Recognition and Enforcement of Decisions Concerning Maintenance Towards Children, and the 1973 Hague Convention on the Recognition and Enforcement of Decisions Relative to Maintenance Obligations. Although numerous associations have urged the United States to join in these treaties, little progress has been made.

COLLECTING ACROSS STATE LINES

First the good news: you do not have to travel to the state where the absent parent resides in order to use the enforcement techniques discussed in this section. The bad news is that these procedures take some time and often involve the use of government services, which can be quite agonizing. This is particularly frustrating where an absent parent skips from state to state. You are urged to "grit your teeth" and perform each task one step at a time.

Uniform Reciprocal Enforcement of Support Act

URESA is the abbreviation for the Uniform Reciprocal Enforcement of Support Act. It is a uniform law that has been adopted by every state in the country, as well as Guam, Puerto Rico, and the Virgin Islands. Put simply, URESA allows you to file a petition for child support in your own state that eventually results in a hearing in the state where the absent parent resides, without the necessity of your presence. It is basically a "two-part" lawsuit and is used exclusively for the collection of back support, current support, modification of support and medical expenses.

To commence an action through URESA, you must apply at your local child support agency (see Appendix A). The government attorney at the local office will process the legal paperwork for you and send it to the child support office where the absent parent resides. The government attorney in that support enforcement office will then file a proceeding in the local courts to enforce the husband's obligation of support. It will greatly expedite matters if you know where the absent parent is residing. They will also require a certified copy of your divorce decree or other support order and you must complete a petition which contains information regarding your case.

The government attorney who receives this information will review it for accuracy and sufficiency and forward it and other documents to the county and state where the absent parent resides ("the responding jurisdiction"). You need not attend any hearings or hire any attorney in the responding jurisdiction. The attorney designated under the responding jurisdiction's URESA statute will act as your attorney on this matter.

If the responding state is unable to locate the absent parent, it will write back to the local office where you applied with any information they obtained. Either you or the local office or both will then attempt to locate a new address or location for the absent parent. If the absent parent lives in the same state, but resides in a different county, the petition will be forwarded to the appropriate county for further proceedings.

Once the absent parent is located, the judge in his area will set a time and place for a hearing on the petition and issue an order for him to appear in court. A copy of the divorce decree or other order of support will be filed in their registry of foreign child support orders (foreign in this case meaning "out of state").

If the absent parent fails to appear in court on the time and date scheduled, the court will enter a judgment against him by default, and collection procedures can be instituted at that time just as if the absent parent was residing in your state. If the absent parent appears and admits the allegations contained in your petition, a support order is entered in that state. If the absent parent appears and denies any duty of support or raises any other kind of defenses, then the court schedules a full-scale hearing similar to a trial.

The court in the responding state may have a hearing with the attorneys and the absent parent prior to trial in an attempt to obtain settlement. Often times the hearings are continued to allow time to obtain further information from the initiating state. You may be required to answer written questions (called "interrogatories") that are submitted by the absent parent or his attorney. You may also be required to answer questions under oath before a court reporter in your state (called "depositions") which will be transcribed and forwarded to the responding court for use in the hearing. While there is no right to a jury trial, the alleged father may be entitled to one if paternity is an issue. Although the government attorney in the responding state may encourage you to attend the hearing, your attendance is not required under URESA.

The most common defense that the absent parents try to raise is the refusal of the custodial parent to allow visitation. Another common defense is inability to pay. These defenses generally carry little weight with the court and often times will not even be considered in determining the obligation of support. More legitimate defenses include non-paternity (the absent parent is not, in fact, the father of the child) or that the child has reached the age of majority. State law varies on the age of majority and the obligation to pay support after the age of eighteen (18). For example, if you live in a state where the age of majority is eighteen (18) and your ex-husband lives in a state where the age of majority is twenty-one (21), you can use URESA to collect child support for the time period eighteen (18) through twenty-one (21) even though that is not the law in your state.

Assuming these defenses are not applicable to your case, a support order will be issued from the responding state and a copy is sent to the initiating state. The court generally requires the absent parent to make regular payments to the court which are then forwarded to the appropriate child support collection office for disbursement to you. If the absent parent fails to make payments that are set forth in the support order, the responding court may take whatever action that is available to them to enforce judgment in their state.

URESA can be used not only to enforce existing support obligations, but also to initiate support. Once the hearing has been had and the support order entered in the responding state, you can bring whatever subsequent actions are necessary in that state either through a private attorney or through the government. You also are not required to use the local government child support office to maintain a URESA proceeding. You may initiate it yourself or use a private attorney.

An alternative procedure available under URESA is the registration of a foreign support order. With this procedure you can even include temporary support orders where you have not yet received a final decree. Basically, you send a certified copy of the order you obtained in your state to the state and county where the absent parent resides. The clerk of that court will record the support order in the registry of foreign support orders. You may register it in the county where the absent parent resides, where he has property, or where he works. The filing of the support order in the registry of foreign support orders constitutes registration. At the time of filing, the court gives the absent parent notice of registration by certified or registered mail. If the absent parent does not contest registration, the registered order is confirmed. The registered foreign support order is then treated in the same manner as a local support order entered by the responding court.

As attractive as this simplified registration procedure appears, I do not advise its use unless you are represented by an attorney. Once the support order is registered in the responding state through this registration procedure, you may waive your right to have modification hearings, visitation hearings, and custody hearings heard in the state where you reside. The majority of courts have held that the absent parent can request modification of the registered order upon a showing of changed circumstances in the responding state because it is treated in the same manner as a local support order. The same is true for custody and visitation provisions. Any such modification of a registered order modifies the original order in your state as well. Therefore, a normal URESA petition with a hearing is greatly preferred because issues such as modification, custody and visitation are not a part of that limited proceeding. Potentially disastrous results can be avoided.

The biggest drawback to the use of the URESA proceeding is the amount of time it takes to go through the whole process. The last matter we handled in California took 14 months from the time of the initiation of the proceeding to the time of the hearing in Southern California. Some states are faster in their processing, but horror stories are rampant throughout the country. As with all areas of government-assisted child support enforcement, it works much better on paper than it does in practice. To minimize the time delay, communicate frequently with both the local support enforcement agency in your state and the office in the responding state as well. If you are still not getting action, contact the United States Senator in both your state and the responding state and send a copy of your complaint to the regional support enforcement office (see Appendix A).

A not infrequent problem is the father who skips from state to state. As soon as he is notified about the URESA hearing, he moves to another state. This kind of activity will require more involvement on your part to keep track of his movements. There are criminal enforcement procedures available through URESA if your particular state or the state where he lives permits criminal non-support actions. Although it is seldom used, you should put pressure on the local district attorney's office to bring a criminal action if he has been skipping around the country to avoid the judicial process. If you can convince the local district attorney to bring an action for criminal non-support, he will be arrested and, hopefully, extradited to your state. You may be asked to pay the costs of extradition. Bear in mind, however, that such a process can be a powerful influence for someone to pay child support. If the contempt proceedings outlined in Chapter 8 cannot be utilized because of constant movement by the absent parent, and you are not otherwise getting anywhere, you should devote all your efforts to pressuring the local district attorney to take some action.

Interstate Income Withholding

If you know the name of the absent parent's employer, Interstate Wage Withholding should be undertaken immediately. Interstate Wage Withholding can be used to collect both current and back child support; it can be done by you personally in some states or by the local child support agency in all states. It can only be used when there is an existing support order. It is not effective against the self-employed or unemployed.

The law of the state where the absent parent is employed governs the exact method of withholding a portion of his pay to apply to your child support. Most of the regulations regarding income withholding pertain to "IV D" cases enforced by the child support enforcement office. It is much easier to use them than to try to do this yourself. They have all the forms and can generally do it just as quickly as you, unlike the URESA procedure described earlier in this chapter. You generally must provide them the following documents:

1. Certified copy of the original court order of support
2. Certified copy of an order of withholding (See Chapter 7)
3. A sworn affidavit from you regarding the amount of the child support arrearage, or a certified copy of the payment record from the governmental agency which collects child support for you.
4. The name and address of the absent parent.
5. The name and address of the absent parent's employer.
6. Where the payment should be sent, if it is not contained in the court order withholding earnings.

Federal regulations require that the local child support enforcement office send prompt notice to the responding state where the absent parent is employed, to begin interstate withholding. The state must initiate withholding when the arrearage totals one month's amount of support, but does have the discretion to set an even earlier date. The responding state must send the absent parent notice of the proposed order withholding earnings and provide the absent parent an opportunity to contest it. It must also notify the absent parent's employer of the income withholding order. If the absent parent terminates employment within the responding state, that state must notify the initiating state of the name and address of the parent's new employer if known.

The child support enforcement amendments of 1984 which set forth the income withholding requirements have been applied inconsistently by the individual states. Some states require registration of a foreign support under URESA or a filing of foreign judgment (discussed below) before enforcing the order by interstate income withholding. This, of course, requires another layer of activity before withholding can commence. Additionally, this requirement of registration forces the custodial parent to risk subjecting herself to jurisdiction of the responding state (a risk explained earlier in this chapter). Such a registration could result in a modification or a change in custody and visitation, which could become binding on the custodial parent in her own state.

In an effort to avoid this problem, the American Bar Association and the National Conference of State Legislatures have enacted the model Interstate Income Withholding Act which has been adopted by numerous states. It eliminates the risk of modification in the responding state since neither the custodial parent or the child reside there. In other words, modification must be sought in your state rather than his.

Briefly, the model act proceeds as follows:

1. The support agency or custodial parent requesting income withholding must send the documents listed above to the income withholding agency of the state where the absent parent is employed. Either a private person, a private attorney, or a government attorney may request withholding. This option is permitted by federal regulations, but is not required, and in some states, such as Texas, only the government agency or another state can request the income withholding.

2. Upon receiving such a request and the documents, the income withholding agency will enter the order in its own

records (if withholding is handled administratively in that state) or with the clerk of the court. Entry is limited to obtaining income withholding and no other purpose.

3. Whoever sends the notice to the absent parent in a state locally will also send notice in the interstate withholding case. The same opportunity to contest withholding in an intrastate case will be provided in an interstate case.

4. At any hearing to contest the withholding, the certified foreign order and statement of arrearages that you have provided in support of the order will constitute prima facie proof of validity of the support orders, that the arrearages are accurate, and that you are entitled to income withholding. The absent parent is then limited to the following defenses:

    a. A mistake of fact;
    b. lack of jurisdiction;
    c. fraud in the obtaining of the order or the statute of limitations.

A continuance can be obtained to obtain further evidence. Just like in the URESA action, provision is made for the presentation of testimony by deposition, written discovery, video tape discovery, and even telephone.

5. If the absent parent does not contest the withholding or fails to prevail at any hearing, an income withholding order will be sent to the absent parent's employer just as in a local case.

Sound complicated? It is. The expertise of the support enforcement agency outweighs the probable time delays and they should be utilized by those of you who fall into this category.

Uniform Enforcement of Foreign Judgment Act

The Uniform Enforcement of Foreign Judgment Act was Congress's first attempt to address the problem of people fleeing the state in which a judgment against them was entered. It requires the existence of a support order and cannot be used to initially establish a support obligation. In those states that have adopted it, however, it provides a simplistic approach to allow you to bring an action to enforce a foreign judgment in another state without the necessity of filing a new and independent action in that state. In order to enforce a support order obligation, the support order must be registered in the state where you are seeking collection. Under the Uniform Enforcement of Foreign Judgment Act, the procedure to record your support order is generally as follows:

1. A copy of the support order is filed with the clerk of the court where the absent parent resides. At a minimum, the support order must be a certified copy and, in some states, it is required to be authenticated. Authenticated means that the clerk of the court and the judge of the court have certified it to be a true copy.

2. A statement by the party or the party's attorney setting forth the name and last known address of the absent parent is also filed with the clerk of the court where the absent parent is located.

3. The clerk of the court mails a notice of filing to the absent parent. This notice includes the name and address of the party filing the foreign judgment and/or that party's attorney in the absent parent's state.

4. The clerk of the court also sends a copy of the judgment (support order) that has been filed, or a notice of filing.

5. Depending on the state, you must then wait 5-20 days after the filing and notice of filing to commence any enforcement action. If no action is taken by the absent parent within the applicable time period, the judgment will assume the status and have the same effect and be subject to the same procedures, defenses and proceedings as if that judgment had been entered in that state originally.

This registration procedure can generally be used only with back child support arrearages. The reason is that the UEFJA applies only to final judgments which is one that is not subject to modification in the state which originally entered it. Child support orders are not a final judgment as to future payments because the orders remain subject to prospective modification upon a showing of changed circumstances. You, therefore, cannot use UEFJA to register and enforce an order for future child support payments; you can, however, for arrearages.

Once the judgment is recorded in the state where the absent parent lives, you can then utilize whatever enforcement techniques are available to you in that state just as if he were in your own state. A sample notice of filing of foreign judgment, together with the necessary affidavits, is set forth on page 176.

Long-Arm Statutes

It is always easier to collect child support in your own state than it is in other states, regardless of efforts to systematize and simplify interstate collection. A great amount of time and energy can be saved if you investigate possible collection in some manner within the state even though the absent parent resides without it. Such a collection procedure is utilized through your states "Long-Arm Statutes".

The discussion of long-arm statutes and "in personam" jurisdiction is so complicated that it fills a semester class for first-year law students. For our purposes, the concept is quite simple: If a company is doing business in your state, no matter how minor or incidental, your state has jurisdiction to order it to do certain things. One of the things that the court can order it to do is pay you child support.

The most common example of the use of long-arm statutes to enforce child support locally is where the absent parent works for an interstate corporation. Even though the absent parent works in another state, you can successfully garnish his wages in your state if the company he works for does business in your state as well. For example, assume the absent parent works in New York for Prudential Life Insurance Company and you reside in Oregon. Rather than trying to use URESA or applying for a foreign judgment in New York, you can simply obtain an order withholding earnings and serve it on the local Prudential Insurance Company office in Oregon. Because the company maintains business activities within the State of Oregon, it legally consents to the laws of Oregon and it must comply with those laws in carrying out the garnishment. Accordingly, it must honor your garnishment even though the absent parent is working out of a branch office in New York.

Although these types of procedures are most common in employer/employee situations, the same argument can be made for interstate banks, brokerage houses, and investment and finance companies. This is also a way to quickly subpoena information that you need to ascertain the possibility of assets within a particular company. If you suspect that the absent parent has a stock brokerage account at, say, Smith Barney, subpoena the local Smith Barney office and request this information and let them go through the channels to get it for you. You save yourself a lot of time and money, and usually get the results much quicker than if you had tried to cross state lines.

Long arm statutes vary from state to state and this technique for getting money or information is not universally accepted. If a business maintains any kind of minimum contacts in your state, however, I would utilize this approach first and see what happens before other methods of interstate collection. Most businesses will err on the side of complying with your request rather than fight on the absent parent's behalf. Nobody likes to go to court, including these large companies, when their own financial security is not at stake. They consider these requests a nuisance and it is easier for them to comply than it is to hire an attorney to fight it, especially if the law is unclear. Use this legal ambiguity to your advantage.

SAMPLE 21: NOTICE OF FILING OF FOREIGN JUDGMENT

IN THE CIRCUIT COURT OF THE STATE OF OREGON
FOR THE COUNTY OF MULTNOMAH

In re the Marriage of:	)	
JANE DOE,	)	No. 5001
Petitioner,	)	NOTICE OF FILING OF
	)	FOREIGN JUDGMENT
and	)	
JOHN DOE,	)	
Respondent.	)	

COMES NOW the petitioner and gives notice to respondent of the filing of the judgment rendered in the Circuit Court of the State of Arizona on June 3, 1993, a copy of which is attached hereto. This notice is given in compliance with A.R.S. § 12-1703(B).

DATED this _____ day of _____, 199_.

_____
Jane Doe, Petitioner

AFFIDAVIT

STATE OF OREGON	)
	) ss.
County of Multnomah	)

Jane Doe, Petitioner, makes this affidavit under oath in accordance with A.R.S. § 12-1703.

On June 3, 1993, judgment was rendered by the Circuit Court of Arizona styled "In re the Marriage of Doe in favor of Jane Doe against John Doe" in the amount of $5,000.

The name and last known address of the Judgment Debtor is as follows:

John Doe
100 River Road
Phoenix, AZ

The name and last known address of the Judgment Creditor is as follows:

Jane Doe
500 S.W. Main
Portland, OR
No part of said judgment has been paid.

SIGNED this 3rd day of August, 1993.

_____
Jane Doe, Petitioner

COLLECTING ACROSS INTERNATIONAL LINES

If the absent parent lives in another country, you've got a real problem on your hands. The federal government has always considered the collection of child support to be a state and local matter and they have been very reluctant to involve themselves in international child support matters. The states, together with private and public agencies, are alone in designing solutions to international child support problems and obtaining recognition of judgments in other countries.

The attitude of the federal government is puzzling, since the Department of Health and Human Services has established the Federal Office of Child Support Enforcement and instituted several new programs such as interstate wage withholding. They have also acceded to three international treaties relating to civil law. However, the most important treaty for families is the United Nations Convention on the Recovery Abroad of Maintenance; it has never been ratified by the United States.

In response to this growing problem, the states have been utilizing URESA and are experimenting with various methods and systems. The basis of utilizing URESA in international situations is through the concept of comity. Comity is where one nation allows or recognizes within its territory the law of another nation. It is not based on a signed agreement or treaty because Article 1, Section 10 of the U.S. Constitution prohibits the state from signing a treaty with another state or with a foreign jurisdiction. The comity arrangement circumvents this prohibition. Basically, the arrangement with other countries involves the same two-state lawsuit found in URESA action between states. The definition of the reciprocating (responding) state is expanded to include "any foreign jurisdiction" where this or "a substantially similar law is in effect".

Implementation of URESA is not worldwide and procedures have been developed in only a few countries to date. What follows is a brief description of each of the countries where this matter has been addressed:

Canada - The Canadian provinces have a commonwealth system that is similar to URESA. The petition is filed in your home state and a provisional order is granted, which is then sent to the province where the court has jurisdiction over the absent parent. A confirmation and the order results in the enforcement and registration of the judgment in that province.

United Kingdom - The United Kingdom has reciprocity with at least 33 states to date. Once again, it is similar to URESA in that the petition is filed in your state and the action is moved to the Commonwealth where a hearing is held and an order obtained.

West Germany - Germany does not have a reciprocal act so arrangements with Germany have been on a very informal basis. It involves working with the staff of the German Consulate and correspondence with responsible officials in the country of Germany. California has been the front runner in this arrangement in conjunction with a semi-private agency, the German Institute for Guardianship. A summary of German law and procedures has been sent to all child enforcement offices in the United States and all should have such information available for reference.

Mexico - Mexico also has no reciprocal act with the United States and has no public agencies with specific responsibilities for child support.

Australia and the Republic of South Africa - Efforts are now being made to set up reciprocal arrangements with these two countries as both are interested in establishing programs with the United States.

Arrangements have also been made with France, Hungary, Sweden, Norway, and Poland. In addition, efforts are being made with Austria, Belgium, Czechoslovakia, Denmark, Israel, Italy, The Netherlands, Portugal, Spain, and Yugoslavia. The Federal Child Support Agency is also considering assuming the role as a central clearing house for arrangements with all foreign countries, as the foreign countries desire to work with only a single United States agency.

The only alternative to working through the child enforcement agency and these reciprocity agreements is to hire an attorney in the country where the absent parent is located. Assistance can be obtained through a local branch of the International Social Services Agency in Geneva, Switzerland. Information is available through the New York branch at 10 West 40th Street, New York, New York 10018. Also, the United States Embassy or the countries' Ministry of Justice may be contacted for information.

If the absent parent living in another country is a member of the United States military services or is a federal employee, you can contact the Federal Office of Child Support Enforcement, Department of Health and Human Services, Rockville, Maryland 20852, or the Office of the General Counsel, Department of Defense, Washington, D.C. 20301. This situation is covered more fully in Chapter 11.

CHAPTER ELEVEN

SPECIAL PROBLEMS:
BANKRUPTCY, THE MILITARY
AND GOVERNMENT EMPLOYEES

There are certain situations you may run into in your quest to collect child support where the normal rules do not apply. If the absent parent is in the military, there are special procedures to follow to withhold his wages, and certain notice provisions are required to execute on personal property. Other federal government employees enjoy certain immunities, and special procedures apply to them as well. Even more common today is the situation where the absent parent files for bankruptcy. Upon such a filing, all the normal collection procedures must cease and a whole new set of procedures takes their place. This chapter will explore the special procedures that allow you to collect child support when you encounter any of these situations.

BANKRUPTCY

If the absent parent files bankruptcy, all collection activity must stop. This rule, called the "automatic stay," has no exception; it stops everyone from pursuing collection activities. It is obtained by the simple filing of a bankruptcy petition. If you willfully violate the "stay" by continuing to pursue collection, you may be liable for damages, attorney fees, and punitive damages, or possible contempt of court.

To continue your collection activities requires permission of the Bankruptcy Court. To obtain such permission, you need to apply to the court for "relief" from this stay. Once this relief is granted, you can then go back to your normal collection activities as before. Such relief from the Bankruptcy Court in child support cases is readily granted by the Bankruptcy Judge, but it is not a procedure that can be overlooked.

There are even exceptions to this, however. To understand the exceptions you need to understand the types of bankruptcy proceedings that are being filed. Most of the time they will fall into one of these three categories.

1. Chapter 7 - Liquidation

Chapter 7 is the type of bankruptcy that most people think of when they think of a typical bankruptcy. In a Chapter 7, a trustee is appointed to take all of the debtor's property that is not exempt. The property, if any, is then sold and the proceeds are distributed to all of the debtor's creditors. All of the debts, except those that are non-dischargeable (including child support), are then discharged and the debtor starts over with a "clean slate".

2. Chapter 11 - Reorganization

Chapter 11 proceedings are rare for individuals and are usually confined to larger companies or corporations. In a Chapter 11, no trustee is normally appointed as the debtor is merely trying to reorganize his company and needs some temporary relief from creditors. The debtor presents a plan of reorganization to the creditors as to how the company is going to pay the debts. If the plan of reorganization is approved, it goes into effect and all parties are bound to the new payment agreement. If it is not approved, it is normally converted to a Chapter 7 and all assets are liquidated and disbursed to the various creditors.

3. Chapter 13 - Wage Earner Plan

Chapter 13 is available only to individuals with a regular income who owe less than $100,000 in unsecured debts and $350,000 in secured debts. It is similar to a Chapter 11 in that the debtor attempts to present a plan to repay his debts to the creditors. Chapter 13 gives him an opportunity to repay the debts over a period of time (typically 36 months) free from harassment from one or more of their creditors. Consent by the creditors is not required so long as it is approved by the Bankruptcy Judge. If the creditors will receive as much money under the plan as they would have under a Chapter 7 (where all assets are liquidated), the plan will normally be approved and the debtor will be able to retain all of his property.

Child support payments are never dischargeable in bankruptcy; if he owed you the money before the bankruptcy, he will owe you the money after the bankruptcy. Where the problem normally arises, however, is how you get paid. In a Chapter 7 Bankruptcy, you file a motion for relief from the stay, which as we have said, is routinely granted. In a Chapter 11 and 13 case, however, relief from the stay may be denied when the debtor has proposed a plan to pay the child support arrearages. If the plan appears to meet the Court's requirements for approval, the Court may find that relief from the stay would undermine the debtor's rights under the Bankruptcy law and deny your motion for relief. In those situations, the absent parent makes a payment to the trustee each month and the trustee would thereupon make the court-approved payment to you.

Keep in mind that the bankruptcy only pertains to debts the absent parent incurred up to the time of the filing of the bankruptcy petition. Child support payments due after the filing are not subject to these rules. Thus, for example, if the debtor filed bankruptcy on May 15, 1993, payments due May 1, 1993, and before would be lumped together as a debt on the bankruptcy petition; collection of those amounts would be subject to the jurisdiction of the

Bankruptcy Court. His next payment, due June 1, 1993, is due and payable on that date and is not incorporated into any bankruptcy plan (except for Chapter 13). The issue becomes whether or not you can pursue normal collection activity for these debts occurring after the filing of the bankruptcy without the necessity of a motion for relief from the stay.

It is recommended that you file for relief from the stay in all situations. Chances are that if he owes you money after the filing of the Bankruptcy petition, he in all likelihood owes you money for obligations incurred before the filing. You should also always file a motion for relief from the stay regardless of the chapter under which the bankruptcy is filed. That way you are insured that you will receive payments through the bankruptcy plan or you will be left free to pursue your own collection activities as before. Filing the motion for relief from the stay guarantees that you will not be forgotten somewhere in the process.

To seek relief from the Bankruptcy stay, you must file a motion with the Court where the bankruptcy case is pending and pay a filing fee of $60. A sample motion for relief is set out on pages 187 and 188. The bankruptcy code provides that a hearing must be held on this motion within 30 days and can be postponed only under very limited circumstances. There is no deadline for the Bankruptcy Judge to rule on this motion, but a decision is usually made at the hearing or shortly thereafter.

Most Bankruptcy Courts have no desire to allow debtors to use the bankruptcy case to avoid non-dischargeable obligations such as child support. If the issues are properly raised by a motion for relief, the Courts will usually not allow evasion to occur. Bring the matter to the Court's attention with the motion for relief so that you may commence or continue your collection activities in the State Courts as before. If the issues involved do not involve any significant bankruptcy rights of the debtor or other creditors, the Bankruptcy Judge is usually more than happy to return these family law issues to the State Courts.

SAMPLE 22: MOTION FOR RELIEF FROM STAY

Jane Doe
555 Main Street
Portland, OR 97204
Telephone: 555-1212
     Pro Per

IN THE UNITED STATES BANKRUPTCY COURT
FOR THE DISTRICT OF OREGON

In Re	)	
	)	Case No.
JOHN DOE,	)	
	)	Contested Proceeding
	)	No.
_____Debtor._____	)	
	)	
JANE DOE,	)	MOTION FOR
	)	RELIEF FROM STAY
Plaintiff,	)	
v.	)	
	)	
JOHN DOE,	)	
	)	
_____Defendant._____	)	

TO: The Honorable _____Bankruptcy Judge:

COMES NOW Plaintiff Jane Doe and moves the Court for an Order for relief from the automatic stay order so that child support may be collected in State Court proceedings from earnings of the Debtor which are not property of the estate.

PLAINTIFF JANE DOE alleges, moves and requests:

1.

That on the 1st day of January, 1993, the above-entitled Debtor, filed a voluntary Petition in Bankruptcy in above-entitled Court and was adjudged a Bankrupt on or about the same date.

2.

The Bankruptcy Court has jurisdiction over this proceeding pursuant to 11 USC § 362.

3.

That the Debtor's Chapter 13 was confirmed by the Court.

4.

The plaintiff was listed as a creditor in the schedules of liabilities filed therein by said Bankrupt and was in fact as unsecured creditor of said Bankrupt at the date of the filing of said voluntary Petition in Bankruptcy in the amount of $3,000.

5.

That the nature of said unsecured debt owing by Bankrupt to plaintiff is child support arising out of an order issued on February 10, 1988, by the Circuit Court of the State of Oregon in and for the City of Portland, County of Multnomah. By the terms of said judgment and order for child support the Bankrupt was to pay $300 per month for the support of the minor child(ren) commencing February 10, 1984.

6.

That plaintiff, a Judgment Creditor of the Bankrupt debtor, received a judgment on February 10, 1984, as set forth in paragraph 5 herein above plus interest thereon.

7.

That the aforesaid Judgment and order is a judgment and order determining defendant Bankrupt debtor's obligation for present child support and past accrued reimbursement of child support and as such is non-dischargeable by virtue of 11 USC § 523(a)(5)(A) as amended, 42 USC § 656(b) as amended, and 42 USC § 602(a)(26).

8.

That between February 10, 1984, and the date Bankrupt filed his voluntary Petition in Bankruptcy, the Bankrupt paid a total of $300 on account of his said on-going above-mentioned, child support obligation and nothing on account of said child support reimbursement arrearage obligation.

9.

That between the date when the Bankrupt filed his voluntary Petition in Bankruptcy and the date of this motion, the Bankrupt has paid a total of $300 on account of his said on-going above-mentioned child support obligation and nothing on account of said child support reimbursement arrearage obligation.

10.

There was due and owing on the date of filing of the voluntary Petition in Bankruptcy by the Bankrupt the sum of $5,000 principal plus interest thereon from February 10, 1984, in child support reimbursement arrearages.

11.

That the Chapter 13 plan of the Debtor makes no provision for child support and for $50 monthly to be applied to the arrears as a general unsecured claim.

12.

The Bankrupt has sufficient income to make the scheduled monthly payment of $300 to the Trustee on the arrearage and also pay said ongoing child support. Due to the automatic stay, plaintiff is unable to enforce the herein above-mentioned order for child support against the earnings and property of the Bankrupt which are not property of the estate.

It is therefore respectfully requested that Plaintiff's motion be granted and the stay order previously imposed be partially vacated insofar as it operates to prevent enforcement by plaintiff of the hereinabove referenced order for child support in the State court against earnings and other property of the debtor that are not property of the estate.

DATED this _____ day of April, 1993.

Jane Doe, Pro Per

If you do file the motion, do not forget to serve a copy on the debtor (absent parent), his attorney, and the trustee. The names of these people and their addresses will be contained in the bankruptcy notice that you receive. If the debtor or his attorney make no response to your motion, relief from the stay will be automatically granted. If they do respond, the court normally schedules a short hearing, often times by telephone. You do not need to say anything at this hearing, but you should be present. Since the Bankruptcy Judge will be familiar with the law, you can in this situation rely on his expertise to make the correct decision. Regardless of what happens, your debt will not be discharged (so long as it was incurred after 1981 when these laws went into effect) and you will be able to either receive a payment through the Bankruptcy Court or be free to pursue your collection activities in State Court.

COLLECTING FROM THE MILITARY

If you are attempting to collect child support from someone who is in the military, consider yourself fortunate. Although the procedures are different, all branches of the military service have strong policies which require their military men and women to provide support to their families. This includes enforcement of military family support policies. Although the military and their attorneys are not usually familiar with support enforcement on the civilian side, they do know how to get action out of a non-paying father who is under their command.

The first step in collecting child support from a military parent is to locate where he is stationed. Not only are there five branches of the military—Army, Air Force, Navy, Marine Corp and Coast Guard—they also tend to move once every three years. To assist in locating your absent military man, you can contact the world-wide locator service and be informed of the member's current duty assignment. Recognize, however, that it frequently takes at least six months for a military member's new duty assignment to be placed on the world-wide locater service computer system.

One way to get around this is to contact the service recruiter in the area where the military person enlisted. For a certain period of time, they will retain the active duty orders on those people for whom they were responsible. A soldier's unit of assignment is considered by the military to be public record. Alternatively, if you know where the soldier is being assigned, contact the installation locater at that installation. All military personnel are required to fill out a post-locater card and, once you know the installation to which the soldier has been assigned, call the general number for that installation and ask for the post-base or installation locater. Then call that locater number and ask for the military person's unit of assignment.

Another strategy to locate the soldier is to contact the local legal assistance office where the soldier is assigned. Each branch of the service has such an assistance program which is not really designed to provide assistance to you or your attorney. Most will cooperate; if they do not, you should advise them that your child is an eligible legal assistance client.

Each branch has its own locater service to get you started. Specific information, including addresses and telephone numbers of these locater services, are listed in Appendix C.

Once you have located the soldier, contact his commanding officer by writing him a letter. In the letter you should set out your name and address, the length of time he has not paid his child support, and his name and service number if you have it. Include a copy of the support order if you have one.

If you have no support order in effect, the military will frequently require the military person to pay support anyway. Generally these situations occur when the husband and wife are voluntarily separated, but no support obligation is in effect. If you find yourself in that situation, you can expect that one-sixth of his gross pay will be allotted to you for one child, one-fourth of his gross pay for two children, and one-third of his gross pay for three or more children. For you and two or more children, they will customarily deduct three-fifths of his gross pay.

If the commanding officer does not help you, you can garnish the absent parent's wages if he is 60 days or more behind in his support payments. This means that a withholding order must be sent to the military by someone authorized to do so, which normally does not include you. You must request this withholding order through your local Child Support Enforcement Agency who will have the necessary application forms. They will forward the information and garnishment to the appropriate branch. You should start receiving regular payments within 60 days after receipt of this information by the military.

Military members receive both "pay" and "allowances" or "entitlements". Allowances are things like reimbursement for living off the base and cannot be garnished.

If you do not get an appropriate response from the soldier's commander, and you do not want to go through the support enforcement agency process, there are other people you may contact. Send a letter to the Inspector's General, the Red Cross, or the Army Emergency Relief within the services. The Red Cross and Army Emergency Relief can provide you with financial assistance and put pressure on the non-supporting soldier. The Inspector's General is even better. Commanders do not like to be told by the Inspector's General that they are not doing their job. Quick action usually results. Finally, consider complaining to your local U.S. Senator who will certainly have someone from his office investigate why nothing is being done. These congressional complaints start at the top of the military ladder and proceed down; a response to the request is produced up the ladder. This is extremely effective in getting some young commander to properly respond to your dilemma.

If the absent parent is retired from the military, there are offices in each military branch which will inform you of any pension benefits that are being received by the retired soldiers. Some of these offices will disclose the information over the phone while others require a written request. When contacting them, have available the full name of the military retiree, his social security number and date of birth, his rank and service number if known, and the approximate dates of service. If you must request this information in writing, be sure and include a copy of the support order.

The addresses and phone numbers of the military offices for this information are contained in Appendix C. The Air Force and Navy will disclose over the phone whether or not a retiree is receiving pension benefits and the amount of the gross monthly retirement pay. The Marine Corp and Coast Guard will respond to written requests for information regarding pension benefits and the amount of gross monthly retirement pay. The Army will not provide any information regarding pension benefits unless they are served with a subpoena demanding the information.

Military pension benefits are subject to garnishment for child support pursuant to federal law. Each branch of the agency has a designated agent for receipt for service of process. Once again, it is suggested that you seek garnishment of military pensions through your local Child Support Enforcement Agency.

SUPPORT ENFORCEMENT AGAINST FEDERAL EMPLOYEES

Amazingly, for a long time you could not even garnish the pay of a federal employee. This resulted in the wives and children of federal employees not receiving the same legal protections afforded all other American women and children. Finally, Congress amended the law in 1974, which for the first time permitted the pay of federal employees to be garnished for child support obligations.

Unfortunately, there are still loopholes and prohibitions with respect to federal money. The first problem is that not all pay is subject to garnishment. You are only allowed to garnish disposable pay after taxes. Some federal employees entitled to claim five exemptions on their tax returns will claim none. This results in a greater amount of monthly income being deducted from their gross pay, which in turn reduces the amount of disposable pay that you can garnish. Also deducted before arriving at disposable pay is any amount the employee is paying into his retirement plan, health benefits, group life insurance, and debts due the United States.

The next problem you may encounter is who to serve with the order withholding earnings. Believe it or not, this has been such a hassle for attorneys in the past that the simple garnishment remedy in these situations is rarely utilized. Listing the information on where to serve the documents would double the size of this book. If you find yourself in this situation, go to the library and ask the librarian to help you find 5 CFR Part 581. In this code of federal regulations will be the address for every designated service of process agent for every executive federal branch agency. Unlike the military, there is no central service of process agent and only by locating the correct federal office can you proceed in your collection efforts.

Once you find the appropriate federal office to serve the writ of garnishment, serve the writ by certified mail, return receipt requested. The responsible office is required to review the writ and any accompanying documents to insure that there is sufficient information to identify the subject of the writ. Included in the information you provide should be the absent parent's full name, the date of birth, social security number, veteran's administration claims number, or civil service retirement claim number, and the specific office where the employee works. If they feel the information is insufficient, they will send it back, often without any indication as to why it is being returned. Also, make sure that you specify that the collection is for back child support or they may send it back.

The next issue will be how much pay of a federal employee can be taken in your garnishment action. Federal law establishes certain provisions, but they are compared with the state law limitations from the state where the writ is issued. Unless state law is more rigid, federal limitations will control. For example, if a federal employee has no second set of dependents (remarriage for example), sixty percent of his disposable pay can be garnished. If more than twelve weeks in arrears, sixty-five percent of his pay can be garnished. Alternatively, if the federal employee has a second family or second set of dependents, only fifty percent of his pay is garnished. If that same federal employee, however, is working in certain states only twenty-five percent of his take-home pay can be garnished unless the Court, for good cause, increases the percentage. If you find yourself in that situation, merely file a motion with the Court to increase the percentage of the garnishment to coincide with federal garnishment laws.

As an alternative to the garnishment procedure, you can send a letter to the supervisor of the civilian employee and request assistance in collecting your support. While there are no specific family support regulations like those in the military, there are, in fact, regulations issued by the office of personnel management which are applicable to your case. In your letter to the supervisor, point out that 5 CFR Part 735.207 prohibits indebtedness of federal employees and subjects them to discipline for failure to honor those debts. Also point out that 5 CFR Part 735.209 prohibits general conduct by a federal employee that is prejudicial to the federal government. Each federal agency has promulgated their own regulations to implement these federal guidelines which can include sanctions against the employee.

There have been cases where an employee was discharged from the federal service for failure to maintain his financial responsibilities "in a matter to preclude the need for garnishment." Normally, for a first offense, the employee will be counselled and given an oral admonition. A second violation could result in a letter of reprimand, and a third offense might bring a suspension from his job without pay. Recognize, however, that when federal supervisors discipline employees for indebtedness, the regulations require there be some connection between the employee job performance and the debt. Facts supporting such a connection would be if the non-support problems are keeping the employee from work or hampering his ability to work. Where the employee is himself a supervisor or has a security clearance, failure to meet these financial obligations could be embarrassing to the government and that, in and of itself, establishes an appropriate connection. This is a further example of the necessity of being a squeaky wheel by continuing to press for payment. If the employee is absent a lot because of the court hearings you schedule, you can bet that it will come to the attention of his supervisor (especially if you have already advised his supervisor of the problems you are experiencing in collection).

The biggest problem in collection in connection with the federal government is not with the federal employees. It is those individuals who contract with the federal government to sell the government products or to perform services of any nature. These "government contractors" get a free exemption from garnishment procedures you would normally follow.

Take a real example. A woman is owed back child support from a man who contracts to sell communication products to the Bonneville Power Administration. Each time the Bonneville Power Administration needs a cellular phone, they contact this man who provides them with a phone system and a bill for services. This contract, which amounts to several thousand dollars monthly, is paid by the same office of the BPA every month.

Logic would dictate that you serve a writ of garnishment on the paying office of the BPA and receive all the funds that would normally be going to the absent parent. Wrong! Because Congress has passed no law allowing you to garnish the federal government under those situations, they are immune from garnishment and will return the garnishment to you without action. Therefore, the absent parent is free to collect those monthly payments from the federal government every month without interference from you.

If you find yourself in this situation, you will have to use the other techniques outlined in this book. The first thing you should do is file a contempt of court action against the absent parent and request the court to order the absent parent to turn those payments over to you, or at least a percentage of them. This puts the onus of directing the payments to you on the absent parent, and eliminates the garnishment problems with the federal government. If he fails to do so, you can request another contempt of court proceeding for failing to follow the order redirecting the payments.

CONCLUSION

CONCLUSION

A
s you can see from reading this book, the road of child support collection is not a smooth one and the process has ample room for improvement. There are wide variations in collection from state to state because of the failure to implement these collection procedures on a federal or interstate level. Much child support remains uncollected; most estimates peg the figure at around $3 billion per year.

Individual states, however, are becoming more and more creative in their collection attempts:

• In Oregon, the Department of Revenue has an ongoing "Ten Most Wanted" list of delinquent fathers. Warrants for their arrest are issued and their faces hang on posters in stores, offices and newspapers statewide.

• In Los Angeles County, they have conducted "Fathers Day Sweeps" which provide delinquent, non-custodial parents with an opportunity to become current in their obligations. This amnesty program resulted in the collection of $800,000 in child support arrearages and more than 20,000 calls from delinquent parents.

• In Massachusetts, collection officers matched names of delinquent fathers against their roster of unemployment compensation recipients and intercepted more than $2 million in benefits. They also scooped money from workers compensation payments.

• New Jersey and California have commenced attaching lottery winnings. New Jersey also garnished $1.2 million from a total $2.5 million intended for plaintiffs in a class action discrimination suit in that state.

The federal government has also proposed legislation to assist in child support collection efforts. In 1994, all child support payments must be withheld from a non-custodial parent's paycheck, even if the parent has a spotless record of making the payments. Also proposed is legislation that presumes that anybody seriously behind in child support payments who moves to another state will be in violation of federal law, even if he moves in order to get a job or to be closer to his child.

These efforts are all fine and dandy. Unfortunately, two fundamental problems continue to exist that will probably never be resolved. You must always keep these problems in mind when either collecting child support for yourself or on behalf of another.

The first problem is when the father does not have the money to pay adequate child support. Many fathers may be unable to provide the support their children need to get a decent start in life, even if they try. One visit to your local courthouse will remind you of how young, unemployed, and unemployable some of these fathers are. You must be realistic about how much support you can expect the father to provide.

I say this not to garner any sympathy for absent fathers, but to point out that you must be financially realistic in your expectations. You "can't get blood out of a turnip" is a true statement in the collection of child support. In many states, the experts—the local child support enforcement agencies—spend as much on child support collection as they collect, and in some cases spend more. In essence, what has been created is a method to transfer income from fathers to government lawyers and employees with no net gain to dependent mothers as a group.

Do not let yourself get into a situation where you are paying out more money than you are collecting. Along the same lines, a little bit of something is better than a whole lot of nothing. It may be better to settle for a lesser amount than to put the absent parent out of business. Carefully compare monthly payments that you can realistically expect, to that one big "hit" where you never hear from the absent parent again. If your actions are going to prevent him from continuing in business, reconsider the aggressiveness of your action and make sure it will produce the best results in the long term. You may have to settle for less than you need and deserve, but remember that you are trying to make the best of a bad situation. Don't let emotion rule your common sense in your eagerness to collect.

This brings up the second problem that should always be considered. Once you attempt to obtain money from another individual involuntarily, that man becomes your adversary and his actions can become unpredictable. The situation can become quite dangerous. Recently, a man walked into a local support enforcement office in one state and gunned down two state employees who had garnished his check to pay child support arrearages. Physical harm to such people is rare, but danger to former wives and girlfriends is not. Trying to collect money under those circumstances often adds fuel to a fire that is already barely under control.

Never underestimate the impact a successful collection will have on the psyche of the person you are pursuing. If you feel there is a danger, you should seriously consider having someone else do the collection for you, regardless of the delay. It is just not worth it to get killed or seriously injured to collect money, and many times you are faced with that risk when you try to collect support by yourself. If you feel you can deal with that risk, then by all means you should pursue collection of child support. Otherwise, get someone else to do it. In any event, be cautious.

Lastly, do not feel guilty about aggressively seeking money from your former husband or boyfriend. He is, first and foremost, a parent. The money you seek is not for you, but for your children. His failure to pay it is a crime. When he purposely evades you and tries to circumvent your effort to hold him accountable, he is harming the interests of your children.

You now have the knowledge to take charge of protecting these interests and the power of the courts to turn this knowledge into action. You are entitled to utilize that knowledge and power for yourself and your children.

Good Luck!

GLOSSARY

Absent Parent: Any individual who is absent from the home and is legally responsible for providing financial support for a dependent child.

Action: An ordinary proceeding in a court by which one party sues another.

Adjudication: The entry of a judgment or decree by a judge after submission of evidence by all parties to the action.

Administrative Agency: An agency of the state or federal government charged with administering particular legislation. Examples are state welfare and state IV-D agencies.

Administrative Determination of Support: A support obligation arrived at as a result of the administrative process.

Administrative Procedure: Method by which support orders are made and enforced by an executive agency rather than by courts and judges.

Affidavit: A written declaration or statement of fact, made voluntarily and con-

firmed by oath or affirmation of the party making it, taken before an officer authorized to administer oaths.

Aid to Families with Dependent Children (AFDC): Assistance payments made on behalf of children who are deprived of the financial support of one of their parents by reason of death, disability, or continued absence (including desertion) from the home; known in many States as ADC, Aid to Dependent Children.

Arrearage: The total unpaid support obligation owed by an absent parent.

Assignment: An eligibility requirement for AFDC whereby the applicant/recipient must assign to the State all rights he or she may have in their own behalf or in behalf of a dependent child.

Assistance: Support money or goods granted to a person or family based upon income.

Comity: The practice by which courts of one State follow the decision or recognize judgments of another although they are not bound to do so; a willingness to

201

grant a privilege to another State out of courtesy, deference, and good will.

Consent Agreement: Voluntary written admission of paternity or responsibility for support.

Custodial Parent: Person with legal custody and with whom the child lives; may be parent, other relative or someone else.

Default: Failure of a defendant to file an answer, response, or appeal in a civil case within a certain number of days after having been served with a summons and complaint.

Default Judgment: Decision made by the court when the defendant fails to respond.

Defendant: Person against whom a civil or criminal proceeding is begun.

Dependent: A person to whom a duty of support is owed.

Deposition: The gathering of written statements from witnesses which are made under oath but not at the court hearing, and to be used later at the trial.

Enforcement: Obtaining payment of a child support or medical support obligation.

Execution: Enforcement of a civil money judgment by ordering a sheriff to seize and sell the judgment debtor's real or personal property.

Federal Parent Locator Service: The system devised and operated by OCSE for the purpose of searching Federal Government records to locate absent parents.

Garnishee: The person in possession of a judgment debtor's property upon whom a garnishment is served.

Garnishment: A legal proceeding whereby a judgment debtor's property or money in the possession of a third person (garnishee) is seized and applied to the payment of the judgment.

Genetic Testing: Analysis of inherited factors (usually by blood test) of mother, child and alleged father, which can help to prove or disprove that a particular man fathered a particular child.

Guidelines: A standard method for setting child support obligations based on the income of the parent(s) and other factors as determined by State law.

Initiating State: The State in which a URESA proceeding is commenced and where the mother is located.

Interstate Case: A case which is filed under a URESA statute or a case which is referred from a IV-D agency in one State to a IV-D agency in another State (i.e., location request, registration of a judgment, etc.).

Judgment: The official decision or finding of a court upon the respective rights and claims of the parties to an action; also known as a decree or order.

Judicial Remedies: A general designation for court enforcement of obligations. More specifically, it relates to the functions of the judges such as contempt, stay of execution, probation, work release, withheld judgment, garnishment, and involuntary wage assignment.

Jurisdiction: Legal authority which a court has over particular persons, certain types of cases, and in a defined geographical area.

Legal Father: A man who is recognized by law as the male parent.

Lien: A remedy that creates an encumbrance on the real property of the debtor.

Long Arm Statute: A law which permits one State to claim personal jurisdiction over someone who lives in another State.

Motion: An application to a judge for an order or ruling.

Non-AFDC Case: A case where an application for child support enforcement has been filed and the family is not receiving public assistance.

Non-Custodial Parent: The parent who does not have primary custody of a child but who has a responsibility for financial support.

Obligation: Amount of money to be paid as support by the responsible parent and the manner by which it is to be paid.

Offset: Amount of money taken from a parent's State or Federal income tax refund to satisfy a child support debt.

Order: Every direction of a magistrate or judge to a person, made or entered in writing, and not included in a judgment.

Paternity Judgment: Legal determination of fatherhood.

Plaintiff: Person who brings an action, complains or sues in a civil case.

Pleadings: Written allegations filed with the court of what is affirmed on one side and denied on the other, disclosing to the court or jury the issue between the parties.

Putative Father: Alleged father. A person who has been named as the father of a child born out-of-wedlock, but for whom paternity has not been established.

Responding State: A state receiving and acting on an interstate child support case.

Service of Process: The delivery of a summons or other notice to the party to whom it is directed for the purpose of obtaining personal jurisdiction over that party.

Show Cause: A court order directing a person to appear and bring forth such evidence as one has, to offer reasons why the remedies in the order should not beconfirmed or executed. A show cause order is usually based on a motion and affidavit asking for relief.

State Parent Locator Service: The organization in a State charged with the duty of locating absent parents for the purpose of establishing and enforcing child support obligations.

Stipulation: An agreement between parties through their attorneys, if any, respecting business before the court.

Subpoena: An official document ordering a person to appear in court or to bring and/or send documentations.

Summons: A notice to a defendant that an action against him or her has been commenced in the court issuing the summons.

Title IV-D: Title IV-D of the Social Security Act is that portion of the Federal law covering the support enforcement program.

Title IV-D Agency: A single and separate organizational unity in a State that has the responsibility for administering the State Plan under Title IV-D of the Act.

URESA: Uniform Reciprocal Enforcement of Support Act - a law which is enacted at the State level and which provides a mechanism for establishing and enforcing support obligations when the non-custodial parent lives in one State and the custodial parent and child(ren) live in another.

URESA Petition: A legal pleading or application submitted through a court of law in an initiating jurisdiction to a court in a responding jurisdiction. The URESA petition shows a duty of support and the likelihood that the responding State mayobtain jurisdiction over the defendant and/or the obligor's property.

Visitation: The right of a non-custodial parent to visit or spend time with his or her children following separation or divorce.

Wage Withholding: Procedure by which automatic deductions are made from wage or income to pay some debt such as child support; may be voluntary or involuntary.

Writ: An order issuing from a court and requiring the performance of a specified act, or giving authority and permission to have it done.

STATE AND REGIONAL CHILD SUPPORT

ENFORCEMENT OFFICES

ALABAMA
Bureau of Child Support
Dept. of Human Resources
50 Ripley
Montgomery, AL 36130
(205) 242-9300

ALASKA
Child Support
 Enforcement Div.
Dept. of Revenue
550 West 7th Ave., 4th Fl.
Anchorage, AK
(907) 276-3441

ARIZONA
Child Support
 Enforcement Admin.
Dept. of Economic Security
P.O. Box 6123/Site Code 776-A
2222 W. Encanto
Phoenix, AZ 85005
(602) 252-0236

ARKANSAS
Officer of Child Support
 Enforcement
Arkansas Social Services
P.O. Box 3358
Little Rock, AR 72203
(501) 682-8398

CALIFORNIA
Child Support Program
Department of Social
 Services
744 P Street/Mail Stop 9-011
Sacramento, CA 95814
(916) 323-8994

COLORADO
Division of Child Support
Department of Social
 Services
1575 Sherman
Denver, CO 80203-1714
(303) 866-5994

CONNECTICUT
Bureau of Child Support
 Enforcement
Dept. of Human Resources
1049 Asylum Avenue
Hartford, CT 06105
(203) 566-3053

DELAWARE
Division of Child Support
Department of Health &
 Social Services
P.O. Box 904
New Castle, DE 19720
(302) 421-8328

DISTRICT OF
 COLUMBIA
Office of Paternity &
 Child Support
Department of Human
 Services
425 "I" Street, N.W. 3rd Fl.
Washington, D.C. 20001
(202) 724-20001

FLORIDA
Office of Child Support
 Enforcement
Dept. of Health &
 Rehabilitative
1317 Winewood Blvd. Bldg. 3
Tallahassee, FL 32399-0700
(904) 488-9900

GEORGIA
Office of Child Support
 Recovery
State Dept. of Human
 Resources
878 Peach Tree N.E.
Atlanta, GA 30309
(404) 894-4119

HAWAII
Child Support
 Enforcement Agency
Department of Attorney
 General
Box 1860
Honolulu, HI 96805
(808) 548-5326

IDAHO
Bureau of Child Support
 Enforcement
Department of Health &
 Welfare
450 W. State Street, 7th Fl.
Towers Building
Boise, ID 83720
(208) 334-5710

ILLINOIS
Bureau of Child Support
 Enforcement
Illinois Department of
 Public Aid
Bloom Building
P.O. Box 19405, 20L.S.
Grand Ave. E.
Springfield, IL 82705
(217) 782-1366

INDIANA
Child Support Enforcement
 Division
Department of Public Welfare
141 South Meridan, 4th Floor
Indianapolis, IN 46225
(317) 232-4885

IOWA
Bureau of Collections
Iowa Department of
 Human Services
Hoove Building - 5th Fl.
Des Moines, IA 50319
(515) 281-5580

KANSAS
Child Support
 Enforcement Program
Dept. of Social &
 Rahabilitation Services
300 S.W. Okaley St.,
Biddle Building
P.O. Box 497
Topeka, KS 66603
(913) 296-3237

KENTUCKY
Department of Child
 Support Enforcement
Department of
 Social Insurance
Cabinet for Human Resources
725 East Main Street,
 6th Floor East
Frankfort, KY 40621
(502) 564-2285

LOUISIANA
Support Enforcement
 Services
Department of
 Social Services
P.O. Box 94065
Baton Rouge, LA 70804
(504) 342-4780

MAINE
Support Enforcement and
 Location
Bureau of Social Welfare
Department of Human
 Services
State House, Station 11
Augusta, ME 04333
(207) 289-2886

MARYLAND
Child Support
 Enforcement Admin.
Department of
 Human Resources
311 W. Saratoga, 3rd Floor
Baltimore, MD 31201
(301) 333-3978

MASSACHUSETTS
Child Support
 Enforcement Unit
Department of Revenue
141 Portland
Cambridge, MA 02139
(617) 727-3950

MICHIGAN
Office of Child Support
Department of
 Social Services
235 Grand Avenue #L406
P.O. Box 30037
Lansing, MI 48909
(517) 373-7570

MINNESOTA
Office of Child Support
Department of Human
 Services
444 Lafayette, 4th Floor
St. Paul, MN 55155
(612) 296-2499

MISSISSIPPI
Child Support Division
State Department of Public
 Welfare
P.O. Box 352, 515 E. Amite
 Street
Jackson, MS 39205
(601) 354-0341, Ext. 503

MISSOURI
Child Support
 Enforcement Unit
Division of Legal Services
Dept. of Social Services
P.O. Box 1527
Jefferson City, MO
 65102-1527
(314) 751-4301

MONTANA
Child Support Enforcement
 Program
Department of Social &
 Rehab. Srvc.
P.O. Box 5955
Helena, MT 59604
(406) 444-4614

NEBRASKA
Child Support
 Enforcement Office
Department of
 Social Services
P.O. Box 95026
Lincoln, NE 68509
(402) 471-9125

NEVADA
Child Support
 Enforcement Program
Department of
 Human Resources
2527 N. Carson Street
Services
Capital Complex
Carson City, NV 89710
(702) 885-4744

NEW HAMPSHIRE
Office of Child Support
 Enforcement Services.
Division of Welfare
Health & Welfare Building
6 Hazen Drive
Concord, NH 03301
(603) 271-4426

NEW JERSEY
New Jersey Div. of
 Public Welfare
Bureau of Child Support
 & Paternity
CN 715
Trenton, NJ 08625
(609) 588-2401

NEW MEXICO
Child Support
 Enforcement Bureau
Department of
 Human Services
P.O. Box 25109
Santa Fe, NM 87503
(505) 827-4230

NEW YORK
Office of Child
 Support Enforcement
New York State
 Dept. of Social Services
P.O. Box 14
1 Commerce Plaza
Albany, NY 12280
(518) 474-9081

NORTH CAROLINA
Child Support
 Enforcement Section
Division of Social Services
Depart. of Human Resources
100 E. Six Forks
Raleigh, NC 27609
(919) 571-4120

NORTH DAKOTA
Child Support
 Enforcement Agency
North Dakota Dept. of
 Human Resources
State Capital
Bismarck, ND 58505
(701) 224-3582

OHIO
Bureau of Child Support
Ohio Dept. of
 Human Services
State Office Tower
30 East Broad Street-27th Fl.
Columbus, OH 43266-0423
(614) 466-3233

OKLAHOMA
Division of Child Support
Department of
 Human Services
P.O. Box 25352
Oklahoma City, OR 73125
(405) 424-5871

OREGON
Recovery Services Section
Adult and Family
 Services Div.
Department of Human
Resources
P.O. Box 14506
Salem, OR 97309
(503) 378-5439

PENNSYLVANIA
Child Support Programs
Bureau of Claim Settlement
P.O. Box 8018
Harrisburg, PA 17105
(717) 783-8729

PUERTO RICO
Child Support
 Enforcement Program
Department of
 Social Services
CALL Box 3349
San Juan, PR 00904
(809) 722-4731

RHODE ISLAND
Bureau of Family Support
Department of Social &
 Rehab. Srvs.
77 Dorance Street
Providence, RI 02903
(401) 277-2409

SOUTH CAROLINA
Child Support
 Enforcement Division
Department of
 Social Services
P.O. Box 1520
Columbia, SC 29202-9988
(803) 737-9938

SOUTH DAKOTA
Office of Child
 Support Enforcement
Department of
 Social Services
700 Governors Drive
Pierre, SD 57501-2291
(605) 773-3641

TENNESSEE
Child Support Services
Department of Human
Services
Citizens Plaza Bldg. 12th
Floor
400 Deadrick Street
Nashville, TN 37219
(615) 741-1820

TEXAS
Child Support
 Enforcement Division
c/o Attorney
 General's Office
P.O. Box 12548
Austin, TX 78711-2017
(512) 463-2181

UTAH
Office of Recovery Services
Department of
 Social Services
120 N. 200 West
P.O. Box 45011
Salt Lake City, UT
                    84145-0011
(801) 538-4400

VERMONT
Child Support Division
Department of Social Welfare
103 South Main Street
Waterbury, VT 05676
(802) 241-2319

VIRGINIA
Division of Support
 Enforcement
Department of
 Social Services
8007 Discovery Drive
Richmond, VA 23288
(804) 662-9629

WASHINGTON
Office of Support
 Enforcement
Revenue Division
Department of
 Social & Health Services
Mailstop HJ-31
Olympia, WA 98504
(206) 459-6481

WEST VIRGINIA
Office of Child
 Support Enforcement
Department of
 Human Services
State Capitol Complex
Building #6, Room 812
Charleston, WV 25305
(304) 348-3780

VIRGIN ISLANDS
Support and
 Paternity Division
Department of Justice
48B-50C Kronprindsens Gade
GERS Complex - 2nd Floor
St. Thomas, VI 00802
(809) 776-0372

WISCONSIN
Division of
 Community Services
Office of Child Support
1 West Wilson St., Rm 382
P.O. Box 7935
Madison, WI 53707-7935
(608) 266-9909

WYOMING
Child Support
 Enforcement Section
Div. of Public Asst. &
 Social Services
State Dept. of Health &
 Social Services
Hathaway Building
Cheyenne, WY 82002
(307) 777-7892

GUAM
Office of the
 Attorney General
Union Bank
194 Hernan Cortez Avenue
Agana, Guam 96910
(671) 477-2036

REGIONAL OFFICES OF THE OFFICE OF
CHILD SUPPORT ENFORCEMENT

REGION I
CONNECTICUT,
MAINE,
MASSACHUSETTS,
NEW HAMPSHIRE,
RHODE ISLAND,
VERMONT

OCSE Regional
Representative
John F. Kennedy
Federal Building
23rd Floor, Room 2303
Boston, MA 02203
(617) 565-2463

REGION II
NEW YORK,
NEW JERSEY,
PUERTO RICO,
VIRGIN ISLANDS

OCSE Regional
Representative
Federal Building, Room 4048
26 Federal Plaza
New York, NY 10278
(212) 264-2890

REGION III
DELAWARE,
MARYLAND,
PENNSYLVANIA,
VIRGINIA,
WEST VIRGINIA,
DISTRICT OF COLUMBIA

OCSE Regional
Representative
P.O. Box 8436
3535 Market Street,
Rm. 4119 MS/15
Philadelphia, PA 19101
(215) 596-1396

REGION IV
ALABAMA,
FLORIDA,
GEORGIA,
KENTUCKY,
MISSISSIPPI,
NORTH CAROLINA,
SOUTH CAROLINA,
TENNESSEE

OCSE Regional
Representative
101 Marietta Tower, Ste. 821
Atlanta, GA 30323
(404) 331-5733

REGION V
ILLINOIS,
INDIANA,
MICHIGAN,
MINNESOTA,
OHIO,
WISCONSIN

OCSE Regional
Representative
105 W. Adams Street 20th Fl.
Chicago, IL 60603
(312) 353-4237

REGION VI
ARKANSAS,
LOUISIANA,
NEW MEXICO,
OKLAHOMA,
TEXAS

OCSE Regional
Representative
1200 Main Tower Building
Suite 1700
Dallas, TX 75202
(214) 767-9648

REGION VII
IOWA,
KANSAS,
MISSOURI,
NEBRASKA

OCSE Regional
Representative
601 East 12th Street
Federal Building, Room 515
Kansas City, MO 64106
(816) 426-5159

REGION VIII
COLORADO,
MONTANA,
NORTH DAKOTA,
SOUTH DAKOTA,
UTAH,
WYOMING

OCSE Regional
Representative
Federal Office Building,
Rm. 1185
1961 Stout Street
Denver, CO 80294
(303) 844-5646

REGION IX
ARIZONA,
CALIFORNIA,
HAWAII,
NEVADA,
GUAM

OCSE Regional
Representative
50 United Nations Plaza
Mail Stop 351
San Francisco, CA 94102
(415) 556-4415

REGION X
ALASKA,
IDAHO,
OREGON,
WASHINGTON

OCSE Regional
Representative
2201 Sixth Avenue
Mail Stop RX-70
Seattle, WA 98121
(206) 442-2775

CHILD SUPPORT ADVOCACY GROUPS
AND STATE-FUNDED GROUPS

ALABAMA

**Association for Child
Support Enforcement
(ACES)**
Judy Hayes,
 Regional Director
#2 Sherwood Forest
Duncanville, AL 35456
(205) 752-8760

ARIZONA

**Organization for Protection
 of America's Children
 (OPAC)**
April J. Skelton
18501 East Bay Road
Higley, AZ 85236
(602) 988-3238

Kathy Gaddy
Chandler, AZ
(602) 899-5056

CALIFORNIA

**Single Parent Action
 Network**
Mary Drummond
10560 Colona Road
Rancho Cordova, CA 95670
(916) 635-9176

**Single Parents United "N"
Kids (SPUNK)**
Susan Speir
5823 Marna Street
Long Beach, CA 90815
(213) 591-3381

Top Priority - Children
Teddy Kieley
P.O. Box 2161
Palm Springs, CA 92263
(619) 323-1559

Gloria Allred, President
Stephanie, Contact
6380 Wilshire Boulevard,
Suite 1404
Los Angeles, CA 90048
(213) 653-8087

COLORADO

**Kids in Need Deserve
 Equal Rights (KINDER)**
Mary Alice Chaffin
5420 Wild Lane
Loveland, CO 80537
(303) 663-0949

Fathers for Equal Rights
(303) 936-3257

CONNECTICUT

**Parents Enforcing
 Court- Ordered Support
 (PECOS)**
Patricia Caputo
23 Indian Run
Enfield, CT 06082
(203) 749-0894

**DISTRICT OF
 COLUMBIA**

National Congress of Men
Washington, D.C.
1-800-366-8786

**Women's Legal
 Defense Fund**
Amy Barrison
 (Child Support)
Suite 400
2000 P. Street, N.W.
Washington, D.C. 20036
(202) 887-0364

FLORIDA

**Association for Children
 for Enforcement of
 Support, Inc. (ACES)**
Southeast Region
Judy Hayes,
 Regional Director
(205) 752-8760

GEORGIA

**Coalition to Help Enforce
Child Support**
Marianna Rich
3056-A Spring Hill Road
Smyrna, GA 30080
(404) 633-9503

ILLINOIS

**Organization for Child
 Support Action (OCSA)**
Mary Wyse
P.O. Box 504
Villa Park, IL 60181
(708) 833-3427

IOWA

**Association for Children
 for Enforcement of
 Support, Inc. (ACES)**
702 Franklin Avenue
Council Bluffs, IA 50312

**Coalition for Child
 Support Enforcement**
631 42nd Street
Des Moines, IA 50312

Fathers for Equal Rights
3623 Douglas
Des Moines, IA 50310
(515) 277-8789

Parents for Child Support
1714 W. 15th Street
Sioux City, IA 51103

MARYLAND

**Organization for the
 Enforcement of Child
 Support (OECS)**
Elain and William Fromm
119 Nocodemus Road
Reistertown, MD 21136
(301) 833-2458

MICHIGAN

ACES
Linda DeMare
815 S. Gargantua
Clawson, MI 48017
Unpublished Number

Fathers for Equal Rights
654 Forrest
East Lansing, MI
(517) 337-0333

Marge Johnson
P.O. Box 40563
Redford, MI 48240
(313) 357-0456

Karen Pattison
915 Lizzie Street
Sault Ste. Marie, Michigan
49783
(906) 632-6364

MISSOURI

**Parents Unified for Lawful
Support Enforcement
(PULSE)**
Pamela Burton, Director
3227 Greenwich
St. Charles, MO 63301
(314) 233-9125 Work
(314) 723-4659 Home

**Association for Child
Support Enforcement
(ACES)**
Jane Stout Van Winkle,
President
P.O. Box 18314
Raytown, MO 64133

**Child Health and
Support Enforcement**
Stephanie Maple
P.O. Box 10005
Springfield, MO 65808
(417) 836-1591 Work
(417) 831-8290 Home

**Citizens Advocating
Universal Support
Enforcement**
P.O. Box 32063
St. Louis, MO 63132

NEBRASKA

**Child Support
Collection Task Force**
Nebraska Commission on the
Status of Women
Betty Peterson
P.O. Box 6162
Lincoln, NE 68106
(402) 471-2039

NEW HAMPSHIRE

**Fathers United for Equal
Justice**
5 Harold Drive
Nashua, NH 03060

Parents for Justice
3 Pleasant Street
Concord, NH 03301

NEW JERSEY

**Camden County Probation
Department**
Mid Atlantic Bank Building,
2nd Floor
Broadway & Cooper Avenue
Camden, NJ 08002
(609) 756-0023

Judy Richter
P.O. Box 1401
Burlington, NJ 08016
(609) 586-6043

NEW MEXICO

**Dads Against
Discrimination**
Albuquerque, NM
(505) 299-2673

NEW YORK

**For Our Children
and Us, Inc. (FOCUS)**
Fran Mattera, Director
550 Old Country Road
Hicksville, NY 11801
(516) 433-6633

Helena Vitale
Brooklyn, NY 11204
(212) 232-6335

Office for Women
Mona Orange, Director
395 Oser Avenue
Hauppauge, NY 11788
(516) 348-5460

OHIO

**Association for Children
for Enforcement of
Support, Inc. (ACES)**
Ms. Jensen
723 Philips, Suite 216
Toledo, OH 43602
**Dayton Family
Service Association**
1714 West Third St.
Dayton, OH 45407
(513) 222-0381

OKLAHOMA

**Association for Children
for Enforcement of
Support, Inc. (ACES)**
Ms. Wright
(918) 492-7335

**Oklahomans Organized
for Child Support
Enforcement**
Debi Evans
3518 E. Virgin Place
Tulsa, OK 74115
(918) 832-1860

OREGON

Child Deserve Support
Gail Esters
150 Kingwood Avenue, NW
Salem, OR 97304
(503) 378-7526
(502) 393-2344

PENNSYLVANIA

**New Jersey Council
for Children's Rights
(NJCCR)**
Ms. Seidel
P.O. Box A
Glenside, PA 19038

SOUTH DAKOTA

**Linda Lea M. Viken,
Attorney**
Member of the House of
Representatives
P.O. Box 3299
Rapid City, SD 57709
(605) 341-4400

TENNESSEE

Gail Forsythe
Forsythe Road
Route 3, Box 42A
Selmer, TN 38375
(901) 645-6387

Parents For Equal Rights
227 Music Square East,
Suite 272
Nashville, TN 37203
(615) 327-8667

TEXAS

**Organization for Child
Support Action (OCSA)**
Deborah Seitzer
24163 Boerne Stage Road
San Antonio, TX 78255
(513) 698-3354

Women's Advocacy Project
1-800-777-FAIR

VERMONT

Legal Aid
151 Elm Street
Montpelier, VT
(802) 223-6377
Vermont for Kids
103 S. Main
Waterbury, VT 05676
1-800-645-5437 (in Vermont)
(802) 341-2740

VIRGINIA

**For Our Children's
Unpaid Support (FOCUS)**
Bettiane Walsh
P.O. Box 842
Vienna, VA 22180
(703) 860-1123

WASHINGTON

POPS
Michael Carrell
10210 Lake Louise Dr., S.W.
Tacoma, WA 98498
(206) 581-2859

211

MILITARY LOCATOR SERVICES

United States Army

Commander

United States Army

Finance and Accounting Center

Attn: FINCL

Indianpolis, IN 46249

(317) 542-2155

(317) 542-2154

(317) 542-4211 Locator Telephone

United States Air Force

Air Force Academy Finance Center

Attn: RPT

Denver, CO 80279-5000

(303) 370-7051

(512) 652-5774 Locater Telephone

United States Navy

Navy Finance Center

Retired Pay Department Code 301

1240 East 9th Street

Cleveland OH 44199-2058

1-800-321-1080

(202) 694-3155 Locator Telephone

United States Marine Corps

Marine Corps Finance Center

Code CPR

Kansas City, MO 64197-0001

1-800-645-2024

(202) 694-1614 Locator Telephone

United States Coast Guard

Commanding Officer

U.S. Coast Guard Pay and Personnel Center

444 Southeast Quincy Street

Topeka, KS 66683

(913) 295-2657

(202) 426-8898 Locator Telephone

INDEX

Administrative Review, 33
Aid to Families with Dependent
  Children (AFDC), 62, 157
attorney fees, 17
Automatic Stay, 181
Bankruptcy, generally, 181-187
Bar Association, 60
blood tests, 13
bonds, 107
Certificates of Deposit, 92
change of circumstances, 33
Child Support
  Enforcement Agency, 13
City Business License, 78
comity, 177
Complaint, 18
contempt hearing, 57
Contingent Fee Agreement, 57
Consent Agreement, 12
City Directory, 73
collection agencies, 3
Contempt Proceeding,
  generally, 126, 139-146
  Motion and Affidavit
    for (Sample 19), 144-146
  Order to Appear for, 146
"cooling-off" period, 19
County Recorder, 17
credit agencies, 64
credit bureau, 88
credit reports, 82
Creditor's Bill, 123-124
criminal records, 79
Decree of Dissolution
  of Marriage, 19
  form (sample 3), 22-23

Default, 19
  Motion and Order of
    (sample 2), 21-22
deputy district attorney, 60
disability, 37
Divorce, petition for, 17, 19
  form (sample 1), 20-21
drivers records, 73-74
earning capacity, 35
Execution, personal property
  (sample 12), 116
  generally 115-121
exemptions, 106-107
Federal Aviation
  Administration (FAA), 95-96
federal employees,
  generally, 190, 194
fifty-dollar disregard, 157
foreign countries,
  generally, 177-179
Freedom of Information
  Request (sample 9), 73
  generally, 72-73
Garnishment, Writ of, 105
  (sample 10), 109
genetic tests, 13
grantor-grantee index, 93
"happy hour", 15
"IV-D" attorneys, 62
interested parties, 121
interrogatories, 166
interstate income
  withholding, 164, 169-172
IRS full collection
  procedure, 155-157

Judgment Debtor Exam,
  generally, 88, 129-139
  Motion for (sample 16), 133
  Affidavit in Support of
    (sample 17), 134
  Order for (sample 18), 135
lawsuits, 94
lien, foreclosure of, 64, 105-106
life insurance, 30
long arm statutes, 164, 174-175
lot block report, 93
medical insurance, 30
Military
  generally, 81-82, 187-190
Modification, Affidavit in
  Support of (sample 6), 44
Modification, Motion and Order
  to Show Cause for (sample 5), 42
Modification Proceedings,
  generally, 33-51
Notice of Demand to Pay
  Judgment (sample 15), 132-133
Notice of Filing of Foreign
  Judgment (sample 21), 176
Notice of Financial
  Responsibility, 150
parent locater services, 83
Paternity Proceeding, 11
personal property records, 78
private investigator, 67
process server, 18
Property Settlement
  Agreement (sample 4), 25
Publication, Motion and Order
  to Allow (sample 8), 67
putative father, 13
real property records, 78

Registration - Foreign
  Support Order, 168
Relief from Stay, Motion for
  (sample 22), 185-186
remarriage, 37
responding jurisdiction, 165
Request for Production
  (sample 7), 45
Secretary of State. 76
Separation Agreement, 17
service by publication, 66
Settlement Agreement, 19, 24
sheriff, 18
spousal support (alimony), 17, 18
statutory guidelines, 18
Sheriff's Instructions
  (sample 13), 119
Subpoena, generally, 125, 126-129
  form (sample 14), 128
  duces tecum, 126
Support Order, 11
tax exemption, 30
tax refund intercept, 64, 153-155
Uniform Enforcement of Foreign
  Judgments Act, 164, 172-174
Uniform Reciprocal
  Enforcement of Support Act
  (URESA), 164, 165-169
utility companies, 74
voter registration, 74
Wage Withholding Orders
  (sample 11), 114
  generally, 64, 113-115, 151-153
Writ of Execution, 105